PENNSYLVANIA

PENNSYLVANIA BY ROAD

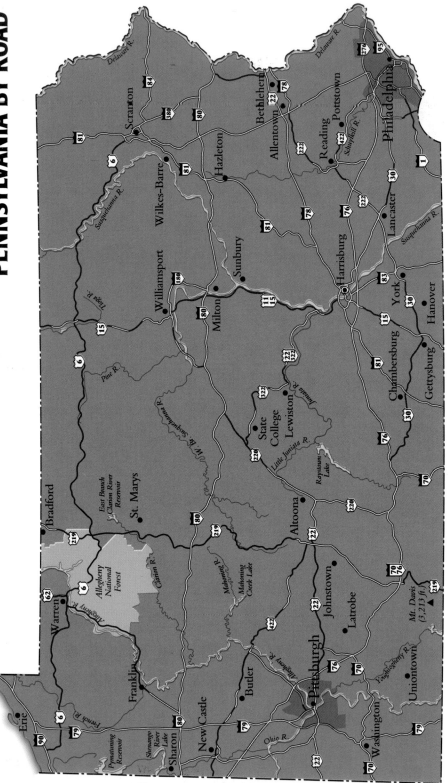

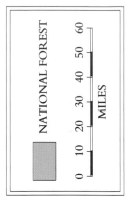

NATIONAL FOREST

MILES

0 10 20 30 40 50 60

N
W E
S

CELEBRATE THE STATES
PENNSYLVANIA

Stephen Peters

BENCHMARK BOOKS

MARSHALL CAVENDISH
NEW YORK

Benchmark Books
Marshall Cavendish Corporation
99 White Plains Road
Tarrytown, New York 10591-9001

Library of Congress Cataloging-in-Publication Data
Peters, Stephen.
Pennsylvania / Stephen Peters.
p. cm. — (Celebrate the states)
Includes bibliographical references (p.   ) and index.
Summary: An introduction to the geography, history, government, economy, people,
achievements, and landmarks of the "Keystone State," Pennsylvania.
ISBN 0-7614-0644-1
1. Pennsylvania Juvenile literature. [1. Pennsylvania.]
I. Title. II. Series.
F149.3.P46 2000   974.8—dc21   99-16414   CIP

Maps and graphics supplied by Oxford Cartographers, Oxford, England

Photo research by Candlepants Incorporated

Cover photo: The Image Bank / Gary Cralle

The photographs in this book are used by permission and through the courtesy of; Blair Seitz : 6-7, 20, 21,
48-49, 53, 55, 59, 61, 65, 70, 72, 74, 105, 113, 119 (top). Photo Researchers, Inc. : Jerry Irwin, 10-11;
Joseph Nettis, 16, 99, 102; Blair Seitz, 19, 56, 62-63, 66, 114, 115; Alan & Sandy Carey, 23(top); Jeff Lepore,
23(bottom), 24, 122 (left); Kjell B. Sandved, 119 (bottom); Tom McHugh, 122 (top); Jeff Greenberg, 138.
Walter Choroszewski : 13, 17, 73, 104, 107, 109, 116, 126. Carnegie Museum of Art, Pittsburgh: Gift of
Mr. & Mrs. Robert McEldowney Jr.: 26-27. Corbis: 45,128,129,131,133,134,137; Peter Harholdt, 29; Wally
McNamee, 47; Bettmann Archive, 37,38,84,86,87,89, 92,94; Robert Maass,79; Michael Nichols, 81(right);
Francis G. Mayer, 81(left); Hulton-Deutsch Collection, 83,132, 135; Lynn Goldsmith, 90. Palmer Museum
of Art, The Pennsylvania State University: 31. The Library Company of Philadelphia: 32-33. Library and
Archives Division of the Historical Society of Western Pennsylvania, Pittsburgh, PA.: 40. Steel Heritage
Corporation, Coordinator of the Rivers of Steel National Heritage Area: 43. Jerry Millevoi : 76-77, 96-97,
back cover. The Image Bank : Michael Melford, 125.

Printed in Italy

1   3   5   6   4   2

CONTENTS

PENNSYLVANIA IS...

Pennsylvania is a scenic place . . .

"Our road wound through the pleasant valley of the Susquehanna; the river, dotted with innumerable green islands, lay upon our right; on the left, a steep ascent, craggy with broken rock, and dark with pine trees. . . . The gloom of evening gave it all an air of mystery and silence which greatly enhanced its natural interest."

—Charles Dickens, writer

"Nowhere in this country, from sea to sea, does nature comfort us with such assurance of plenty, such rich and tranquil beauty as those unsung, unpainted hills of Pennsylvania."

—Rebecca Harding Davis, writer

. . . rich in natural resources.

"By Heaven, Thompson, I've discovered an empire."

—Captain James Potter, early settler and explorer

"Pennsylvania coal is what made this country run!"

—Tom Rusin, coal miner

Pennsylvania is historic . . .

"I never liked history before I moved to this little town, but I do now. You've got early German settlers, the stagecoach line, and the Underground Railroad all right here."

—Sarah Gavazzi, restaurant owner

It is "the cradle of toleration and freedom of religion."

—President Thomas Jefferson

. . . and it is a great place to call home.

"My dear sir, if you are as happy in entering the White House as I shall feel on returning to Wheatland Pennsylvania, you are a happy man indeed."
—President James Buchanan to future president Abraham Lincoln

"Pennsylvania? I think of the rolling hills, the countryside, and meadows and streams . . . factories that made us what we are . . . the strong work ethic and sense of family."   —Jim Boyce, teacher

"It's the greatest state in the Union!" —Mike Wilk, antique dealer

---

Pennsylvania is a place of mountains and valleys, rivers and forests, industry and culture. Many people who are born there stay and spend their lives close to home. Others come back after having seen something of the world. It is a place where you can walk through hundreds of years of American history in the morning and enjoy the best of the twentieth century in the afternoon.

1 RICH LAND, NATURAL BEAUTY

Pennsylvania's variety of natural landscapes resulted from dramatic changes in the earth's crust over millions of years. Its mountains and valleys, rivers and rich farmland tell a story of continents shifting on the earth's surface and crashing into one another, of vast inland oceans and ancient swamp forests, and of mountains rising and then eroding over the eons. These changes on the earth's face explain the rich deposits of natural resources beneath Pennsylvania's surface and why Pennsylvania became this country's industrial heartland. They also explain why it is still such a beautiful place.

UNDER THE GROUND

What is under Pennsylvania is as important to its history as what is above ground. Between 600 and 270 million years ago, much of Pennsylvania lay beneath oceans. Materials from the land washed into the shallows of these oceans, while shells and the remains of life-forms collected farther out to sea. A combination of pressure from the water and the earth's internal heat then turned the materials into rock. This rock can be seen in the farmhouses, barns, and churches of Pennsylvania today. At other times in the ancient past, vast swamp forests covered much of the land. Heat and pressure turned the plant matter that piled up in these swamps over

More than 20,000 years ago, glaciers created this twelve-foot-deep rock layer at Boulder Field National Landmark in Hickory Run State Park.

millions of years into coal. A similar process produced the state's oil fields. Coal and oil formed the basis for much of Pennsylvania's, and the nation's, wealth and industry.

RIDGES, VALLEYS, AND FARMS

The Appalachian Mountains that run through Pennsylvania once stood 20,000 feet high. Rain, rivers, streams, and glaciers worked

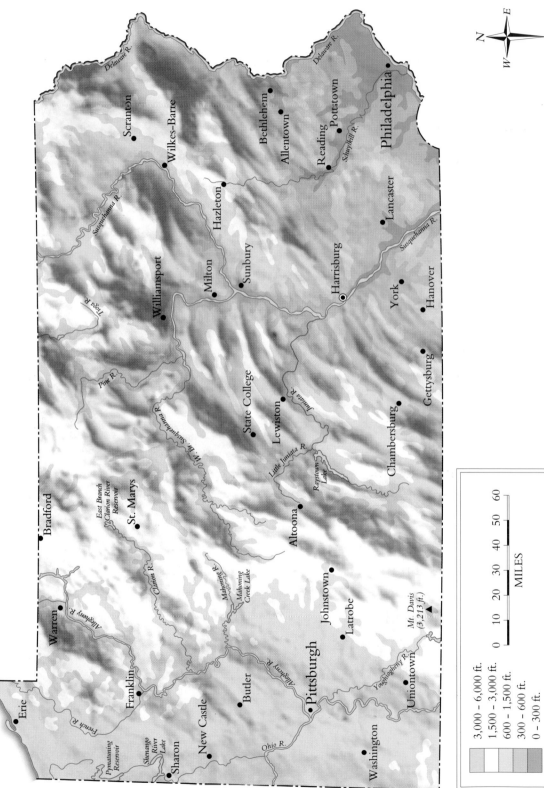

LAND AND WATER

Delaware R.

Delaware R.

Scranton

Wilkes-Barre

Bethlehem

Allentown

Reading

Pottstown

Schuylkill R.

Philadelphia

Susquehanna R.

Hazleton

Lancaster

Susquehanna R.

Tioga R.

Williamsport

Milton

Sunbury

Harrisburg

York

Hanover

Pine R.

State College

Lewiston

Juniata R.

Gettysburg

W. Br. Susquehanna R.

Little Juniata R.

Raystown Lake

Chambersburg

East Branch Clarion River Reservoir

St. Marys

Bradford

Clarion R.

Altoona

Mahoning R.

Mahoning Creek Lake

Johnstown

Latrobe

Mt. Davis (3,213 ft.)

Warren

Allegheny R.

French R.

Franklin

Butler

Allegheny R.

Pittsburgh

Youghiogheny R.

Uniontown

Erie

Pymatuning Reservoir

Shenango River Lake

New Castle

Ohio R.

Washington

Sharon

| 3,000 – 6,000 ft. |
| 1,500 – 3,000 ft. |
| 600 – 1,500 ft. |
| 300 – 600 ft. |
| 0 – 300 ft. |

MILES

0   10   20   30   40   50   60

over millions of years to wear down these mountains. The result is today's varied landscape.

The southeastern part of the state, between the Delaware River and the first ridges of the Appalachians, is known as the Piedmont. It is some of the richest natural farmland in the world. Though the cities of Philadelphia, Reading, Bethlehem, and Allentown have developed here, the region is still the state's agricultural heart. Indeed, the rolling countryside between Philadelphia and Harrisburg is a land of farms. It is home to many Amish, religious people who live without modern conveniences. Amish horses and buggies roll past miles of wheat and cornfields and colorful stone and painted wood barns.

West of the Piedmont lies the Ridge and Valley Region, an area of long valleys and ridges running like a backslash across the state. Driving the winding road over one of these ridges and then dropping down into another valley is sometimes like entering a new world. Some of the smaller valleys are home to industry; drab factory towns nestle into the hills. Others, like Big Valley, are broad and covered in immaculate Amish farms. You may see more horses and buggies on the roads than cars, and the bearded men and bonneted women may look like they live in an earlier century. Driving into Stone Valley you'll find miles of unbroken forests and endless dirt roads. If you see any people at all, they will likely be hunters, fishers, or hikers. Stopping atop Tussey Mountain as you leave Stone Valley, you look down into Penns Valley, in the very center of the state. Here there is good farming as well as excellent hunting, fishing, and hiking. "I love this place," says Paul Kelly, a longtime resident of Penns Valley. "I can hike and camp or I can work in my garden."

Lancaster County is famous for its immaculate and well-tended Amish farms. This part of the state, the region known as the Piedmont, boasts rich soil ideal for farming.

At the western edge of the Ridge and Valley Region is the 1,500-foot Allegheny Front. This long, steep slope of rock, or escarpment, serves as a border to the next region, the Allegheny Plateau. Hawks, falcons, eagles, and ospreys migrate along the Allegheny Front in the fall.

The Allegheny Plateau is a tableland that slopes off across western

Pennsylvania and into Ohio. Much of it has been cut and eroded by winding streams and rivers, so the roads twist and turn through the forests and factory towns in roller-coaster fashion. A popular area for outdoor activities, the Laurel Highlands in the south support many ski resorts, and in the north the vast wild areas of Allegheny National Forest offer miles and miles of skiing and snow-

Lovers of the outdoors enjoy Allegheny National Forest for its camping, hiking, snowmobiling, and fishing. Visitors can walk through old-growth forest, and if they are at the right place at the right time, may catch a glimpse of black bears, deer, beavers, and raccoons in their natural habitat.

mobiling trails. Because much oil, gas, and coal lies under the plateau's surface, it is the center of Pennsylvania's heavy industry.

THREE GREAT RIVER VALLEYS

Three great river systems—the Delaware, Susquehanna, and Ohio—shaped the region's earliest settlement and were important in the development of Pennsylvania's transportation and industry.

The Delaware cuts the jagged eastern border of the state, zigzagging south through narrow rapids and wide, slow spots from New York to the shipping ports of Delaware Bay at the Atlantic Ocean. In the middle of the state, with east and west branches forming a tree on the map, is the Susquehanna River. A favorite among tubers and white-water enthusiasts, the Susquehanna follows a meandering course through the mountains, ending its journey in the Atlantic Ocean at Chesapeake Bay. The Ohio River forms where the Monongahela and Allegheny Rivers meet at Pittsburgh and eventually flows into the Mississippi.

A SEASON FOR EVERYONE

Pennsylvania enjoys four distinct seasons. In winter, the temperature ranges from below zero to the thirties. Many residents can't wait for winter each year, so they can get out to sled, ski, or snowmobile. Although driving the icy mountain roads of central and northern Pennsylvania is sometimes difficult, the views are worth it. The snow-covered forests and countryside are so beautiful they look as if they were painted.

On its way to the Atlantic Ocean, the Susquehanna River carves its way through the forested mountains of central Pennsylvania.

Spring brings abundant rainfall and glorious blooms of yellow forsythia and redbud trees. Throughout spring and summer, azaleas, rhododendrons, trilliums, jack-in-the-pulpits, dogwoods, elderberries, honeysuckles, black-eyed Susans, and mountain laurels bring splashes of color to the state's forests, fields, and roadsides. In summer the temperature rarely breaks 100 degrees Fahrenheit, but the humidity is often high, and residents complain about it constantly.

But no one ever complains about the fall, when the trees turn color. "I went to college in Vermont, which is famous for its fall colors," said Katherine Maleney, who lives outside of Philadelphia, "but the first time I came home for fall break I could hardly believe my eyes everything was so beautiful. I love the way you get the gold-

"There is nothing as magical as a Pennsylvania forest after a snowfall," says Pennsylvania native Irene Eisenhut.

Pennsylvania's many hardwood trees provide plenty of material for a universal children's game: playing in leaf piles in the fall. "I rake them up," says Randy Meyers, with a sigh. "Then the kids scatter them around. Then I rake them up again."

enrod and the asters, not just the leaves. I love the way the plants and all the different trees blend in the fall. The other seasons are good here, too, but I like fall best."

FLORA AND FAUNA

Pennsylvania has a great variety of plant and animal life. Nearly 60 percent of the state is covered in forest. Most of the state's trees are deciduous (they lose their leaves) rather than evergreen. At the time the first Europeans came to America, the state had many four-hundred-year-old trees. Though nearly all of this old growth is now gone, a few stands of virgin forest still remain in the Allegheny National Forest and Cook Forest State Park. Today, forests of maple, beech, and hemlock grow in abundance on the northern Allegheny Plateau. Ash, aspen, cherry, hickory, birch, oak, poplar, sycamore, and red and yellow maple do well in the south.

Animal life is varied, too. White-tailed deer, wild rabbits, black and gray squirrels, raccoons, beavers, foxes, mink, opossums, skunks, and woodchucks roam the state. Slightly less common, but still to be found around forest cabins and campsites, are black bears. Rarer still are wildcats, which live in some remote areas of the state. The Indiana bat, once common in Pennsylvania's more than one thousand caves, is now endangered.

In addition, 373 species of birds have been seen in Pennsylvania. At night in the countryside, you often hear screech, great horned, and barred owls. In the woods are ruffed grouse, two-foot-high wild turkeys, and bobwhite quail. Canada geese and mallard ducks are common on lakes and ponds. Great blue herons nest in the state's northwest corner, and songbirds are abundant in yards and meadows everywhere.

The state also has many kinds of fish, reptiles, and amphibians. Bass, catfish, and sunfish are common. Many of the state's streams are excellent places to catch trout, and you will find northern pike, walleye, bluegill, muskellunge, and black crappie in the lakes and reservoirs.

While Pennsylvania's reptile family includes a number of harm-

Black bears, though generally shy, sometimes make their presence known around rural homes and vacation cabins.

The quavering whistle of screech owls can be heard late at night from orchards and small wood-lots.

THE BOG TURTLE: AN ENDANGERED SPECIES

Bog turtles earn their name because they like to live in bogs, swamps, and marshy meadows with slow-moving streams. There they feed on a variety of plants and animals—insects, berries, and even the flesh of dead animals. When in danger, they burrow into the mucky bottoms of streams.

But development and the selfishness of collectors have made the bog turtle an endangered species. As people drain wetlands for houses, shopping centers, and highways, these rare turtles lose the habitat necessary for their survival. Bog turtles also face pressure from reptile buffs, who value them for their distinctive orange spots, and because, at just 4 to 4.5 inches long, they are one of the smallest turtles in North America.

To prevent further loss of this rare species, the state has persuaded many landowners where bog turtles live to leave the land in its natural condition. And before the state begins a construction project, conservationists review it to ensure that the turtles' habitat is protected.

less snakes, it also includes three poisonous species: the copperhead, the timber rattlesnake, and the eastern Massasauga rattlesnake. The state is also home to wood, eastern box, and bog turtles. One amphibian that lives in Pennsylvania is the hellbender salamander. Pollution watchers pay close attention to this two-foot-long creature, because it is extremely sensitive to pollution. Wherever it is found the water must be clean.

Since the first white settlers came to Pennsylvania, the buffalo, native elk, moose, and timber wolf have disappeared from the state. The state's list of extinct species includes twelve mammals, twenty-seven fish, six birds, two reptiles, and one amphibian. The greatest danger to the remaining wildlife in Pennsylvania is the risk of destroying their habitat by building parking lots, shopping malls, and houses, which are crowding out its many woodlands and rich farmlands. Since the 1950s, Pennsylvania has lost more than four million acres of farmland. When woodlands are cut down and fields are covered over, the natural ecosystems are ruined. A growing number of Pennsylvanians believe now is the time to act to prevent more loss of their natural world.

Although conservationists have reintroduced bald eagles, river otters, and Yellowstone elk into Pennsylvania's ecosystem, much work remains to be done. Jennifer Ottinger, a staffer at Hawk Mountain Sanctuary, says, "We need to have respect for all other beings in our world. That includes plant life and insects as well as other animals." Ottinger and many other Pennsylvanians have made this their life's work.

2 THE KEYSTONE STATE

Mountain Stream, by George Hetzel

If you look at a map of the original thirteen American colonies, you will see that Pennsylvania is in the middle. It appears to hold the others in place, much like the "keystone" that stonemasons put in the middle of an arch to hold the others together. Because of this, Pennsylvania has been nicknamed the Keystone State, and in fact it has played many key roles in American history. Americans declared independence, wrote the Constitution, set up a national capital, established heavy industry, and decided the course of the Civil War in Pennsylvania. They also put the American ideal of religious tolerance into practice there before anywhere else.

NATIVE PENNSYLVANIANS

When the first Europeans set foot in Pennsylvania, 20,000 Native Americans already lived there. Early European settlers reported that Native Americans in Pennsylvania were generally tall, and some historians say that they probably were, because they seem to have had a better diet than Europeans at that time. They grew and ate corn, squash, and beans, but their diet also included potatoes, wild peas, maple syrup, wild plums and grapes, cranberries, strawberries, hickory and chestnuts, and blackberries.

Three groups of Native Americans lived in Pennsylvania. The Monongahela people settled along the rivers of western Pennsylvania.

An explorer with a special talent for exaggeration, Captain John Smith depicted the Susquehannocks as "a Giant like people" on this map. They impressed him greatly "both in language and attire."

Because they disappeared about the time the first European settlers arrived, we don't know much about them. It is possible that other native groups drove them away or that the diseases the Europeans brought wiped them out. The Susquehannocks lived south of the mountains along the Susquehanna River, about halfway across the state. A people with a strong military and trading tradition, they surrounded their villages with stockades, tall fences to keep out wild animals and enemies. Inside these stockades, the Susquehannocks lived in longhouses, buildings where several families lived side by side along a central passageway. The third group, the Leni-Lenape, had the lands south of the Kittatinny Mountains along the Delaware River and on the Piedmont. In 1698, Pennsylvanian Gabriel Thomas wrote that the Leni-Lenape leaders were "slow and deliberate, . . . naturally wise, and hardly to be out-witted."

PENN'S WOODS

The first European settlers in present-day Pennsylvania came under the Swedish flag in 1638. They made a lasting contribution to the American frontier by introducing the log cabin. However, their small community near present-day Philadelphia, called New Sweden Colony, soon came under the control of Holland. The European powers were struggling over North America, and both Sweden and Holland lost out early. In 1664, not long after Holland took control of New Sweden, it fell under English rule.

At about this time, the English king Charles II owed a large sum of money to Sir William Penn, who had recently died. This meant that he now owed the money to Sir William's son, also named William. William had recently converted to a new Protestant sect called the Religious Society of Friends. People called them Quakers because they were said to quake and tremble when they rose to speak in their religious service, which they called Meeting. The Quakers, or Friends, did not have ministers. Instead, each person might be called by the Holy Spirit to speak in Meeting. They also did not believe in taking oaths or in violence. That meant that they absolutely refused to serve in armies. Many people disliked the Friends for holding these beliefs, so they were persecuted.

William Penn wanted to establish a haven where people like the Quakers could practice their religious beliefs freely. So, he asked that the king settle the debt by giving him a large piece of land in

This painting by Benjamin West shows William Penn and Native Americans making a treaty under an elm tree at Shackamaxon, "the place of the chiefs," in 1682. The Quakers and the Native Americans swore, in Penn's words, "Kindness and Good Neighborhood, and that the Indians and the English must live in Love."

the New World. His colony would be open to people of all faiths. He called it his Holy Experiment. Charles agreed. In 1681, he granted Penn a large tract of land. Penn wanted to name it Sylvania, Latin for "woods," but the king insisted on honoring Penn's father

When Peter Cooper painted this view of Philadelphia in 1717, Pennsylvania's first city was

by naming it Pennsylvania, "Penn's woods." In 1682, Penn and a group of Quakers sailed from England and established the city of Philadelphia ("City of Brotherly Love" in Greek).

Penn's colony grew from 500 in 1682 to around 20,000 at the start of the 1700s. From the beginning, the Holy Experiment attracted a variety of people. In 1683, a large group of Germans settled just north of Philadelphia. Their leader, Francis Daniel Pastorius, wrote that "no one shall be disturbed on account of his belief, but freedom of conscience shall be granted to all inhabitants of the province."

Another religious group, the Moravians, moved into the Lehigh Valley in 1741. Like the Quakers, they had refused to conform to the state church at home. Other nonconforming groups included the Mennonites and Amish, who settled the Susquehanna Valley

on its way to becoming a major urban center.

and the rich farmland in Lancaster County. They and other German settlers came to be known as the Pennsylvania Dutch. This does not mean that they came from Holland. The "Dutch" is for "Deutsch," the word for "German" in the German language.

Many Presbyterian Scotch-Irish came in the 1600s, settling around present-day Harrisburg. Thousands of Irish came, too. In fact, around 1740 in Ireland, people sang a popular song called "Off to Philadelphia" about going to Pennsylvania. In 1773 alone, 162 ships from Ireland landed in Philadelphia.

But not all people came to Penn's Holy Experiment freely. The ship *Isabella* carried 150 slaves to Philadelphia in 1684. Though Quakers, Mennonites, and African Americans later worked together to abolish slavery, Quaker merchants were as guilty as anyone of profiting from the slave trade.

And while William Penn treated the Indians fairly, his successors did not. In the Walking Purchase of 1737, for example, the Leni-Lenape agreed to give away the amount of land a person could walk in one day. The colonists, however, cheated by hiring professional runners to run in relays, covering much more land than the Leni-Lenape thought they were giving away.

By 1750, Philadelphia had become the most important city in the British colonies. Despite its shortcomings, it was a forward-looking place with many firsts to its credit: the first written objection to slavery in America was the Germantown Protest of 1688; Thomas Bond and Benjamin Franklin founded the first hospital in the colonies in 1751; the Society for the Relief of Free Negroes Unlawfully Held in Bondage, the first organization working to end slavery in America, began in 1775.

FRONTIER VIOLENCE

But as Pennsylvania grew, the struggle to control the riches of North America continued. In the early 1700s, France controlled Canada and its lucrative fur trade. To extend that trade, in the 1750s they began building forts along the southern shore of Lake Erie, in English territory. However, because of their religious beliefs, the Quaker-controlled government of Pennsylvania refused to participate in military action to protect British claims. The colony of Virginia therefore sent troops under George Washington with a letter demanding that the French leave British territory. The French commander refused and, within a year, the French and Indian War began.

The French were eventually driven out, but violence between the

BENJAMIN FRANKLIN: SCIENTIST, AUTHOR, FOUNDING FATHER

In 1723, a teenaged Benjamin Franklin arrived in Philadelphia from Boston. He had little money at the time, but he would eventually become the city's most prominent citizen. A printer by trade, Franklin worked hard and bought a newspaper, the *Pennsylvania Gazette*, in 1729. A few years later he began publishing *Poor Richard's Almanack*, a book full of useful information and the witty sayings of "Poor Richard." "Early to bed and early to rise makes a man healthy, wealthy, and wise" and "Fish and visitors stink after three days" were two of these sayings. Franklin wrote them himself, though many people thought Poor Richard actually existed. Nearly every house in the colonies bought a copy of the *Almanack*. The book made him famous.

Franklin also earned a reputation as a scientist, experimenting with electricity and inventing bifocals, a more efficient stove, and swimming fins. Though he only had two years of formal schooling, he was given the title Doctor and led the University of Pennsylvania.

As a member of the Continental Congress, Franklin helped edit the Declaration of Independence, written by his friend Thomas Jefferson, and traveled to France to enlist French help in the Revolution. Because the French loved *Poor Richard's Almanack*, they received him warmly and Franklin made many new friends for the American cause. At the end of the Revolution, Franklin negotiated peace with the British and then returned home.

When he died at age eighty-four, he was so loved and respected that 20,000 people attended his funeral.

European settlers and the Native Americans continued after the war. In one incident, a group of settlers from Paxton Township attacked a camp of peaceful Conestoga Indians in Lancaster County, killing six of them. When the survivors were taken to the Lancaster workhouse for protection, the Paxton Boys, as the attackers were called, struck again and murdered them. Many people in the colony supported the Paxton Boys. Others were disgusted. Prominent Philadelphian Benjamin Franklin called the Paxton Boys "savages."

A NEW NATION

The French and Indian War had been expensive, and to pay for it England levied heavy taxes on the American colonies. People in America thought this unfair because they had no representation in the British parliament. The cry "No taxation without representation!" went up.

In 1774, colonial leaders chose Philadelphia, then the largest city in the colonies, as the meeting place for the First Continental Congress to discuss their grievances with England. Two years later, Philadelphia became the birthplace of the United States when, on July 4, 1776, the Second Continental Congress approved the Declaration of Independence.

England was determined to fight for the colonies, and in the late summer of 1777, British forces began marching toward Philadelphia. George Washington led the newly formed Continental army out to stop them at Brandywine Creek, west of Philadelphia, but the British won the battle and occupied the city. Washington led his troops north to Valley Forge and settled in for the winter.

Lacking adequate boots, many of the soldiers wrapp[e]
in rags. Washington wrote that "you might have track[e]
. . . by the blood of their feet." About 3,000 of Washing[to]
soldiers died of typhus, smallpox, and pneumonia d[uring]
winter. It seemed the army would fail.

But Washington held his army together through the bitter cold
despite meager food supplies. A small group of sympathetic Europeans—Prussian Baron Friedrich von Steuben and Frenchman
Marquis de Lafayette among them—helped turn the army into a dis-
ciplined fighting force and train the troops in the latest battlefield

*In 1776 the Second Continental Congress voted to declare independence from
England in Philadelphia. "We must all hang together, or assuredly we shall all
hang separately," said Benjamin Franklin after the signing.*

George Washington's army suffered terrible hardships through the winter at Valley Forge. Men did whatever they could to stay warm, even sometimes wrapping rags around their shoeless feet. Many did not survive, but those who did formed an effective force that eventually defeated the British.

strategies. In the first battle after Valley Forge, the Continental army shined.

After the Americans won the Revolutionary War, Pennsylvania played an important role in the new nation. Philadelphia served as the nation's capital from 1790 until 1800, and the major route west was through a huge gap in Pennsylvania's Appalachian Mountains. Settlers poured across Pennsylvania, and an atmosphere of progress and innovation followed. In 1794, the first major hard-surfaced road in the country opened, the seventy-mile-long Philadelphia–Lancaster Turnpike which was paved with stone and gravel. Robert Fulton developed a practical and widely copied steamboat in the early 1800s, and the skill of Philadelphia shipbuilders allowed Pennsylvania's merchants to reach far beyond their borders.

In this energetic atmosphere the "canal fever" of the early 1800s began. Mules pulled barges along a system of canals that had been built between economic centers. The system cut the difficult Philadelphia-to-Pittsburgh trip from a month by wagon to five days by canal.

Of course one huge obstacle stood in the way of building a canal from east to west: the 1,500-foot Allegheny Front. An ingenious feat of engineering solved this problem. Crews loaded canal boats onto tracks and from there a steam-powered pulley system hauled them to the other side of the mountain, where they were put back into the water of the connecting canal. After crossing the Allegheny Front this way in 1842, English author Charles Dickens wrote, "Occasionally the rails are laid upon the extreme verge of a giddy precipice; and looking from the carriage window, the traveler gazes sheer down, without a stone or scrap of fence between, into the mountain depths below." Thousands of settlers crossed the mountains this way.

THE CIVIL WAR

By 1860, tensions over slavery in America led a group of Southern states to leave the Union and form their own, separate country

A canal system greatly reduced travel time between Philadelphia and Pittsburgh, but to cross the Allegheny Front canal boats had to be loaded onto a railroad car and carried over the mountain.

called the Confederate States of America. However, newly elected president Abraham Lincoln stood firm against the breakup of the country. The Civil War to preserve the Union began, and once again, Pennsylvania played a key role.

Pennsylvania's highly developed iron industry supplied three-quarters of the cannons used by the Union army. But the state's geography also helped decide the war in which 340,000 Pennsyl-

THE ROBIN HOOD OF CENTRAL PENNSYLVANIA: A LEGEND

When central Pennsylvania was still frontier, a likable young man appeared there. When he visited pioneer farms, he was polite, helped with the chores, and told funny stories. And after he'd left, his hosts often found a pile of money with a note signed "David Lewis, the highwayman."

People began to tell stories about this man who robbed from the rich and gave to the poor. One story told of a posse searching through the mountains for him and meeting a cheerful fellow who said he'd actually seen David Lewis. He and the sheriff struck up such a pleasant conversation that the sheriff suggested maybe the fellow ought to join them, which he did. The young man listened as the sheriff talked nearly the whole time about his wife and children. After the posse got home, the sheriff received a letter signed "David Lewis, the highwayman." In it Lewis thanked the sheriff for being such good company, wishing good health to each member of the sheriff's family.

Like many outlaws, Lewis was finally captured, and he died in jail. What became of his money? He always said he could see where he'd hidden it by looking out the Bellefonte jailhouse window. Some say he stored all his gold and jewels in a deep cave in the mountains. They say you enter this cave and cross a huge underground lake to find the treasure. Although many have looked, no one has found his riches.

vanians served. Confederate general Robert E. Lee wanted to invade the North and strike a blow to the Union's industrial heartland. To do that, he led his army up the Shenandoah Valley of Virginia into Pennsylvania. When a small contingent of his troops ran into part of the Union army, the most decisive battle of the war, the Battle of Gettysburg, began. Beginning on July 1, 1863, the two great armies fought in the fields and woods outside Gettysburg. On the third day of fighting, Lee launched a desperate effort to break the Union center. General George Pickett led between 12,000 and 15,000 men across open fields straight into massed Union troops. Pickett's Charge failed. When he retreated, more than half his men had been killed, captured, or wounded.

Tillie Pierce, a young girl living in Gettysburg, fled the town with her family on the battle's first day. Although they were seeking safety, they nevertheless ended up very close to the fighting. Tillie and her sisters helped care for the wounded soldiers. "On this evening," she said of the second day, "the number of wounded brought to the place was indeed appalling. They were laid in different parts of the house. The orchard and space around the buildings were covered with the shattered and dying, and the barn became more and more crowded."

In all, 50,000 soldiers were either killed or wounded at Gettysburg. When General Lee retreated to Virginia, his line of hospital wagons stretched seventeen miles. Though the war continued, the South had lost its last chance for victory.

The following November, the U.S. government established a national cemetery on the battlefield. The organizers asked President Lincoln to say "a few appropriate words" at the dedication, though he was not the main speaker. His speech lasted only three minutes and received little applause, but the Gettysburg Address has since been hailed as one of the greatest speeches of all time.

LABOR AND INDUSTRY

After the war, Pennsylvania continued to be a key industrial state, producing oil, iron, steel, coal, and other products. Andrew Carnegie built giant steel factories in Pittsburgh, where his workers did hard, hazardous work for little pay.

At the same time, coal increasingly fueled industries and heated homes. Waves of immigrants from Ireland and eastern and southern Europe poured in to work in Pennsylvania's booming coalfields and factories. This work presented unbelievable dangers. Men went into the mine shafts with open flames to light their way, and if they encountered gases, the chances of devastating explosions were great.

A "puddler" working his furnace. This was an extremely hazardous task, because molten ore "puddled" out when the furnace door opened and sometimes flowed out faster than the puddler could get away.

Often mines caved in. Between 1870 and 1900, an estimated ten thousand Pennsylvania miners were killed at work. This does not include those injured or those who died of black lung disease from breathing coal dust. Like the steelworkers, the miners were paid little and had no financial security in case of injury. Though the steel and coal industries benefited the country, the price the workers paid to keep it running was cruel.

In 1892, workers at Carnegie's Homestead Steel Works went on strike when management announced changes in wages. Because Carnegie was in Europe at the time, Henry Clay Frick, his partner, handled the crisis. Frick refused to negotiate with the steelworkers' union. Instead, he brought in strikebreakers and an army of private detectives. The Battle of Homestead followed. For a whole day, workers fought the detectives and strikebreakers before the National Guard stopped them. In all, ten people died, many were wounded, and the strikers were forced back to work at lower wages. Not until much later did they form a union that could successfully bargain with management.

For the coal miners, progress came after John Mitchell organized the United Mine Workers Union (UMW). In 1902, UMW miners went on strike in the eastern Pennsylvania coalfields. The long strike continued into the winter. Many people around the country needed coal from eastern Pennsylvania to heat their homes, and supplies were low. Because President Theodore Roosevelt deemed this a national problem, he stepped in and named a mediator. It was the first time presidential power had been used to settle a labor dispute. Where national interests are at stake, presidents continue to intervene in labor conflicts today.

"Breaker boys" worked deep in the mines alongside grown men before child labor laws put an end to the practice. They faced death or injury from accidents, fires, cave-ins, and black lung disease from breathing coal dust.

THE TWENTIETH CENTURY

When the United States entered World War I in 1917, the Philadelphia shipbuilding industry produced the ships needed to fight the war. Thousands of men joined the armed forces, and the steel and coal industries supplied the industrial muscle needed to win.

Beginning in 1929, however, the Great Depression put as many as three out of four Pennsylvanians out of work. Whole families stood in long lines for hours just to get something to eat. "Even in bitter cold winter they waited," says Adelaide Haller, who lived through that time. "The bread lines stretched down the blocks and around the corner. Sometimes you couldn't even see where they ended."

The Great Depression ended when the United States entered World War II in 1941. Pennsylvania's steel mills, coalfields, and shipbuilding industries again played an important role in the nation's war effort. Pennsylvania also contributed hundreds of thousands of men and women to the armed forces and the defense industries.

Since the end of World War II, the state's economy has changed dramatically. Many steel mills closed in the 1970s, again putting workers on the unemployment rolls and bringing hard times to industrial towns.

Then, in a moment that frightened nearly everyone, the nation's most serious nuclear power accident occurred at Three Mile Island near Harrisburg in March 1979. Because of a technical malfunction and some bad decisions, the plant's nuclear core overheated, and contaminated gas escaped into the atmosphere. On the third day of the accident, as many as 100,000 people began evacuating the area, fearing a complete meltdown and disaster. Eight days later the plant went into cold shutdown, the crisis ended, and most citizens returned to their homes. However, health problems in the area led many local residents to file suit against the company. And many people around the country instantly became antinuclear activists. Others, though, felt the accident led to more dependable safeguards in the nuclear power industry.

Three Mile Island will always be remembered as the site of the nation's worst nuclear power accident.

Today, Pennsylvania's economy continues to reinvent itself as jobs in high-tech and tourism replace those in heavy industries. Agriculture remains strong. With an evolving economy and abundant natural and human resources, Pennsylvania's outlook for the twenty-first century is bright.

3 THE COMMON WEALTH

The capitol in Harrisburg

Pennsylvania is a commonwealth, which means that it is a state founded for the common good of the people. It adopted its present constitution, the fourth in its history, in 1874.

The Pennsylvania Constitution begins with a Declaration of Rights much like the Bill of Rights in the U.S. Constitution. Added to this in 1971 was an amendment prohibiting discrimination based on sex. The state then adopted the Natural Resources and the Public Estate amendment in 1972. This states that "the people have a right to clean air, pure water, and to the preservation of the natural, scenic, historic, and esthetic values of the environment."

INSIDE GOVERNMENT

The constitution goes on to describe the structure and duties of the three branches of government: legislative, executive, and judicial.

Legislative. The legislative branch, known as the general assembly, has two bodies, the house of representatives and the senate. The 203 members of the house are elected for two-year terms, while the 50 members of the senate are elected for four-year terms. The general assembly drafts bills that become laws if they pass both bodies and are signed by the governor.

Executive. The governor, who is elected to a four-year term, heads the executive branch. The governor is responsible for reading all the bills passed by the general assembly and then either vetoing (saying

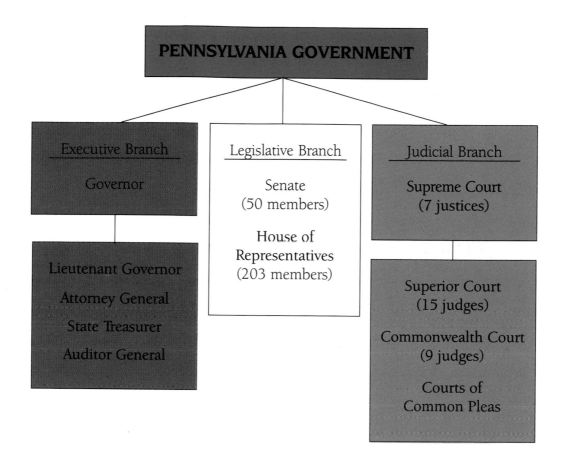

PENNSYLVANIA GOVERNMENT

Executive Branch

Governor

Lieutenant Governor

Attorney General

State Treasurer

Auditor General

Legislative Branch

Senate
(50 members)

House of
Representatives
(203 members)

Judicial Branch

Supreme Court
(7 justices)

Superior Court
(15 judges)

Commonwealth Court
(9 judges)

Courts of
Common Pleas

no to) them or signing them into law. The governor has the right to veto the entire bill or to pick out only certain parts to veto. Unless both bodies of the general assembly vote by a two-thirds majority to override the governor's veto, the bill will not become law.

Other executive officers include the lieutenant governor, attorney general, auditor general, and state treasurer, who are also chosen in statewide elections.

Judicial. The judicial branch interprets the laws by trying people accused of crimes and by settling disputes called civil cases. The supreme court is the highest court in the state. Seven justices sit on the supreme court, each elected for ten-year terms. They review cases ranging from those involving the death penalty to those where a lower court has ruled a state law unconstitutional.

The superior court and the commonwealth court are both statewide courts with judges who are elected for ten-year terms. The superior court hears civil and criminal appeals from the courts of common pleas in each county. The commonwealth court hears only civil cases that involve the state.

EDUCATION AND THE ENVIRONMENT

Education and the environment will dominate Pennsylvania politics into the next century. Pennsylvania allows parents to educate their children at home, and the number of families doing this has grown in recent years. One reason families choose this path, called home schooling, is that they want their children to be taught in a religious atmosphere. Because of the American tradition of keeping church and state separate, public schools cannot do this. Some families also believe that discipline has broken down in the public schools, and they do not want their children to learn bad habits. Although some people oppose home schooling because they fear it will weaken the public schools, others, such as Jim Boyce, a sixth-grade teacher in Pottsgrove, disagrees. He thinks the competition is good. "After all," he adds, "we want parent involvement in education, and this would definitely give parent involvement! Parents who send their children to public schools can learn something from home schoolers."

State representative Ben Ramos sees bilingual education, a teaching system that uses both English and the student's native language, as an important issue. With more and more Spanish-speaking students living in Pennsylvania and with the arrival of Vietnamese, Thai, and Cambodian immigrants, he thinks that schools need to accommodate different cultures and languages. According to Ramos, bilingual programs often do not receive adequate funds. Because of this, they sometimes don't do as good a job as they might, which provides an excuse to give them even less money. "I came to Pennsylvania from Puerto Rico when I was

Asian Americans are an important part of Pennsylvania's diverse culture.

fourteen," says Ramos. "I'm a product of bilingual education, so I know it works. But you have to give it adequate funds."

Taking care of the environment will also remain an important issue for some time to come. Pennsylvania has made real progress in this area. For example, Pittsburgh, once known as the Smoky City because of the air pollution from its many factories, now rates as one of the country's best places to live, and the air is clear. But heavy industry left behind "brownfields," abandoned industrial sites contaminated by hazardous waste. These areas need to be cleaned up before they can be used again.

Pennsylvania's Land Recycling Program works to make these sites safe again and to return them to productive use. York's Industrial Plaza illustrates the success of this program. Built as a manufacturing center in 1908, it lay abandoned from 1958 to 1995, its windows broken and weeds growing through the pavement. Worse, dangerous chemicals polluted the ground. Asbestos made even breathing the air in the buildings dangerous. Today, however, it has been cleaned up and now houses twenty-four businesses.

EARNING A LIVING

Pennsylvania has a diverse and growing economy, one that is changing with the times. The three big sectors of the Pennsylvania economy are agriculture, tourism, and industry.

Riders of the Pittsburgh Duquesne Incline catch a great view of the city's skyline.

Even the youngest farm children have chores. Here a nine-year-old feeds milk to a holstein on a Lancaster County farm.

Agriculture. About 800,000 Pennsylvanians are employed in one way or another in agriculture, furnishing products that range from beef and chickens to fruit and timber. Dairy farmers produce 10.6 billion pounds of milk annually, making the state the fourth-largest milk producer in the country. With 66 million gallons produced annually, Pennsylvania is the second-biggest maker of ice cream and it leads the nation in pounds of mushrooms grown. The horse-breeding industry is also important in Pennsylvania.

SHOOFLY PIE

The Pennsylvania Dutch are famous for their delicious food—delicious and not likely to keep you skinny! A favorite is the sweet, tasty, and oh-so-fattening shoofly pie. It probably got its name from the flies that loved its sweetness (and had to be "shooed" away) as much as people did. Everybody has a favorite family recipe. Have an adult help you with this one.

  1 cup flour
  ⅔ cup brown sugar
  1 tablespoon shortening
  1 teaspoon baking soda
  ¾ cup hot water
  1 cup molasses
  1 egg, beaten
  1 9-inch unbaked pie shell

Combine the flour and brown sugar and then cut the shortening into the mixture until it gets crumbly. Set aside. Dissolve the baking soda into hot (but not boiling) water. Combine the molasses, egg, and baking soda water into a small bowl and beat it well. Pour this into the pie shell and sprinkle with the flour-sugar mixture. Bake at 375 degrees for 35 minutes.

Although 50,000 farms are spread across the state, small farmers are having an increasingly hard time. "The small dairy operators I know get shaved pretty close," says retired farmer Dick Fye, "with the price of equipment and feed going up and the price they get for their products going down. The really big operators are the only ones making it today."

Tourism. In recent years, tourism has grown faster than any other sector of Pennsylvania's economy. It is easy to see why so many people visit the state. Its many ski resorts attract visitors when the snow flies, and major historical sites all over the state lure tourists all year long. In addition, visitors can enjoy excellent fishing, hiking, and camping. Many people visit the state on business, and the opportunity to watch major sports or hear world-class orchestras in Philadelphia or Pittsburgh attracts others. Shoppers flock to the outlet stores of Reading, and vacationers enjoy family fun at amusement parks like HersheyPark near Harrisburg.

GROSS STATE PRODUCT: $357 BILLION

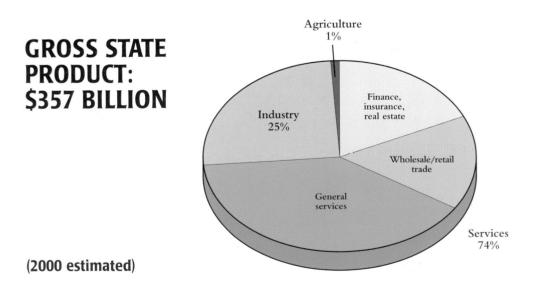

Agriculture
1%

Finance, insurance, real estate

Industry
25%

Wholesale/retail trade

General services

Services
74%

(2000 estimated)

Hikers get their bearings along a trail in Pine Grove State Park.

Industry. Though manufacturing and mining do not play the central role in Pennsylvania's economy they once did, they still account for about 25 percent of the state's economy. Manufacturing takes place mainly in Pittsburgh and in the eastern cities of Philadelphia, Bethlehem, Reading, and Allentown. Transportation equipment, electronics, printed materials, fabricated metals, industrial equipment, and food products are all made in Pennsylvania. The state is first in the nation in production of snack foods like potato chips, pretzels, and processed chocolate and cocoa, and it is still a major producer of coal.

EARNING A LIVING

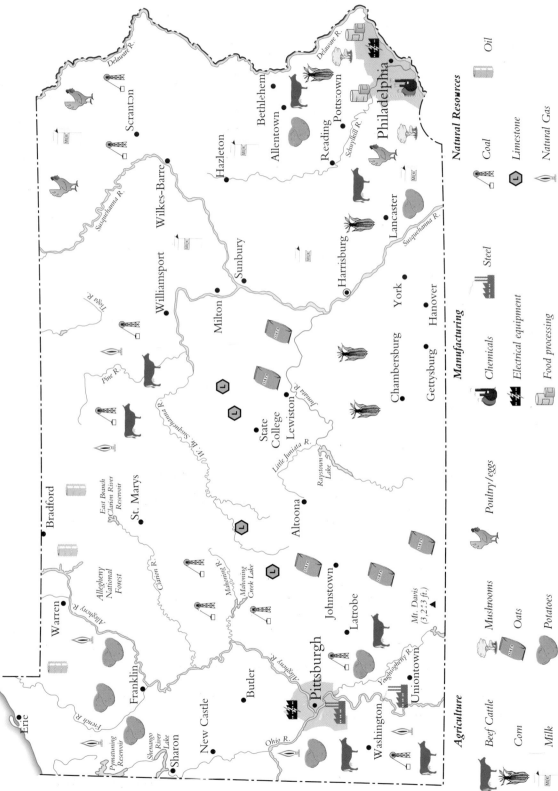

Natural Resources

Oil

Coal

L Limestone

Natural Gas

Manufacturing

Steel

Chemicals

Electrical equipment

Food processing

Agriculture

Beef Cattle

Corn

Milk

Mushrooms

Oats

Potatoes

Poultry/eggs

Lititz, Pennsylvania, calls itself the birthplace of the pretzel, and many residents swear pretzels handmade in Pennsylvania are more delicious than any others.

Pennsylvania's economy has been changing rapidly, but some areas and groups have been left behind. This can be seen in the once-thriving mill and mining towns around the state. In the 1970s many of their factories and mines closed down. Now the towns are in transition, and leaders are looking for ways to breathe new economic life into them. Though tourism has replaced many of the lost jobs, the problem is not likely to be completely solved soon.

The state faces many challenges, but Pennsylvanians don't seem discouraged. "With urban, suburban, and rural components of the state working together," says state senator Jeffrey Piccola of Dauphin County, "nobody can beat us."

4 A STATE OF FRIENDS

Pennsylvanians take pride in all their state has to offer and, of course, its most valuable resource is its people themselves. In Pennsylvania, you will encounter folks with fascinating backgrounds and passions. Some focus their energy on remembering their heritage, others on improving their community today, and still others on just enjoying life.

ETHNIC DIVERSITY

From the original settlement of Penn's Holy Experiment, Pennsylvanians have been a diverse lot. Today, if you ask some of the 12 million Pennsylvanians where their ancestors came from, you will get a riot of answers. The largest single group, however, traces itself back to Germany. The next largest group thinks of itself as Irish, followed by Italian and English. African Americans number about one million, 90 percent of whom live in the Philadelphia area. Today there are also more than 500,000 Jewish people living in the Philadelphia area. More than 300,000 Hispanics live in Pennsylvania, mostly in the eastern part of the state. The majority come from Puerto Rico. "They see opportunity here and that's why they come," says Judy Delgado of the Philadelphia Hispanic Chamber of Commerce. "There are over 7,500 small businesses owned by Hispanics in the Delaware Valley."

Philadelphians love a good time and often, as in this Fourth of July parade down Roosevelt Boulevard, take their community celebrations outside.

Smaller eastern European communities—Poles and Ukrainians, for example—can be found in towns where heavy industry once thrived. Reverend Arthur Turfa, pastor of a Slovak Lutheran church in Lansford in eastern Pennsylvania, says, "People are still very proud of their heritage here. We don't use the language in the service anymore, except for when we sing a certain hymn at Christmas. But a number of the older people can still speak the language, and we keep the recipes alive at home and whenever we have church

THE OLD ORDER AMISH

Imagine living without modern conveniences. No car, no television, no VCR. You might not even have a telephone. Instead of going away to a camp in summer, you stay home and work on the farm. You milk cows by hand. You weed the garden. You help cut hay in the fields and stack it in the barn. Or you help cook and serve food to the many young and not-so-young helpers. There is always plenty of good food and plenty of hard work to do. For fun, you play in a creek or go with your parents to the sale barn, where cattle is bought and sold. You are finished with school after the eighth grade, and then you go to work on the farm.

That's what life might be like if you were born into the Amish community. The Amish are a deeply religious people who live on beautiful farms throughout Pennsylvania and the Midwest. Descended from a German-speaking Swiss religious group, they do not believe in using modern conveniences because they feel closer to God if they live a simple, plain life. They have lived much the same since joining William Penn's Holy Experiment around 1741.

ETHNIC PENNSYLVANIA

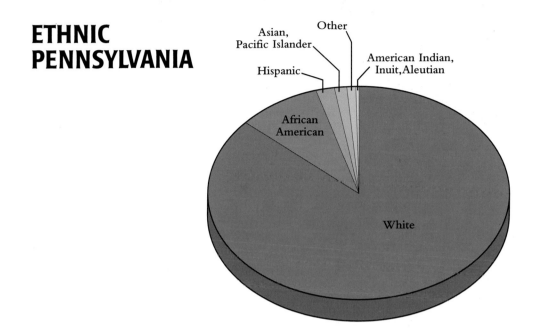

Asian, Pacific Islander

Other

Hispanic

American Indian, Inuit, Aleutian

African American

White

suppers. People always bring holubky [noodles and cabbage] and pierogis [stuffed dumplings]." Indeed, pride in Pennsylvania's ethnic diversity is alive and well.

COMMUNITY INVOLVEMENT

A high percentage of Pennsylvanians—80 percent—who are born in the state still live there. This means that they care about where they live and have a real stake in it.

Pennsylvanians' deep commitment to their community shows in a number of ways. The Quaker influence is one. Philadelphian Thom Jeavons explains why Quakers traditionally engage in social action: "We struggle," he says, "to make our faith relevant and to give it expression."

In the Friends Work Camp Program, volunteers help out in Philadelphia's inner city. They have been doing this since the 1930s. In a typical work camp, suburban or rural people spend time living in the inner city doing home repair alongside homeowners. A project may include painting, repairing damaged walls, or laying linoleum on a kitchen floor. While the "campers" work, they get to know about life in the city. "It is an effort," says program director Katherine Maleney, "to create peace through understanding and working together."

Another organization, Concerned Black Men, got its start in

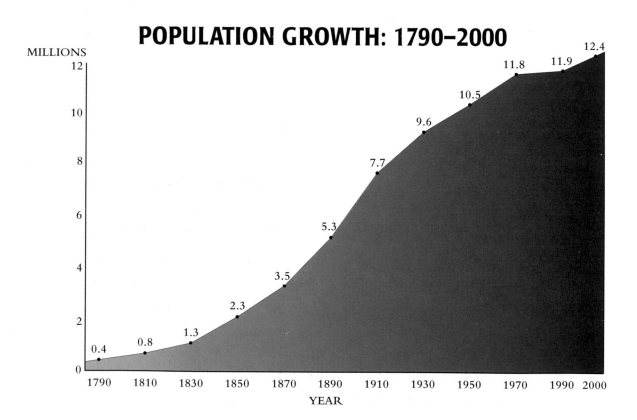

POPULATION GROWTH: 1790–2000

THE BRIDAL DANCE OF WESTERN PENNSYLVANIA

Some eastern European customs have been adapted into marriage celebrations in western Pennsylvania.

One is the rollicking "bridal dance." In this custom, the wedding guests line up to dance with the bride. Each gets a brief turn with her, and then the next person takes over. Those who have danced with the bride join hands and dance in a circle around her. Each new person joins this circle until all the guests are holding hands and dancing around the bride. At a large wedding, hundreds of people will surround the bride.

Then, in the most exciting moment, the groom enters the room and tries to break through the circle to his new wife. He is stopped, however, by a group of his friends and wrestled to the floor. They then lift him over their heads and he is carried hand-over-hand across the heads of the guests and given to his bride. He picks her up and carries her off to the honeymoon as everyone cheers.

Philadelphia but is now nationwide. Five African-American police officers wanted to overcome the negative stereotypes some Philadelphians had of young people. They wanted to highlight all the positive and creative contributions young people were making. Concerned Black Men encourages young people to be proud of their heritage, take good advantage of educational opportunities, and live socially conscious lives.

In Philadelphia the organization offers scholarships, college tours, a program for adults to mentor boys and girls, a science program, and even a rowing team. All the adults are volunteers.

A grandfather and his grandson enjoy a close moment at a picnic.

"We have had many success stories," says Fred Caliman, president of the Philadelphia chapter. "For example, one of our members, a school librarian, noticed a young man who kept coming into the library every day, working really hard. Well, eventually, the librarian found out that this student and his family were homeless, living in their car. Our volunteer took an interest and got him involved in our programs. When this youngster graduated from high school, he won all-city honors. Now he's at the Wharton School at the University of Pennsylvania. And this is just one of many success stories."

ENTHUSIASTIC ABOUT SPORTS

Watch the lines of cars driving through the mountains of central Pennsylvania on a weekend when Penn State's Nittany Lions play football. Then walk through the huge parking lots around Beaver Stadium and smell the barbecues of the tailgaters. You will then see how much Pennsylvanians love their sports teams.

Pennsylvanians enthusiastically support football's Eagles and Steelers, baseball's Phillies and Pirates, hockey's Flyers and Penguins, and basketball's 76ers.

People in Pittsburgh often argue that Pittsburgh is a bigger sports town than Philadelphia—though Philadelphians don't like to hear it. Pittsburghers like to remind the rest of the state that their Steelers have won the Super Bowl four times. They also boast that the Pittsburgh area has produced some of the country's greatest quarterbacks, including Jim Kelly, Joe Namath, Joe Montana, Dan Marino, and Johnny Unitas.

Some Pennsylvanians would rather participate in sports than watch them. On weekends and during vacations, they go white-water rafting, kayaking, or canoeing on rivers and streams. Or they enjoy a hike on one of the state's many trails. Some enjoy spelunking—exploring caves—and others like to spend their free time on one of the state's hundreds of golf courses or many ski slopes.

Fans jam Three Rivers Stadium in Pittsburgh to see the hometown Steelers play in the National Football League.

FRIENDLY FOLK

Ask people in the state to describe Pennsylvanians, and the most common answer you will hear is that they are friendly. Maybe this is one reason the state's tourist industry has grown so quickly. Also, Pennsylvania has a large rural population, and many people believe that country folk are more friendly with strangers than city folk.

"You Have a Friend in Pennsylvania" used to appear on the state's license plates, and this still seems to be true everywhere you go in the state. Just stop on the street and ask one of the locals a question. Chances are you'll fall into a conversation.

Janine Heinser and her husband moved to Mansfield in northern Pennsylvania from Long Island, New York, where they grew up. "We came up here to visit," she said, "and we fell in love with it because everybody is so friendly and laid back. We also thought it would be a good place to raise our kids."

Her friend Mary Wivell, who moved to rural Pennsylvania from Maryland, agrees. "People in Pennsylvania are very friendly and out-

Rafting on the Lehigh River brings a thrill a minute and a welcome break from the everyday routine.

Shirley and Terry Womer and their son Scott show off their cow at their farm in Middleburg. "Farming is a good way of life, but there's not much money in it," says Terry. "The best part of it, though, is that you can be with your family every day."

going," she said. "If you ask directions, they'll help you. Why, I've had people actually say, 'Follow me and I'll show you where it is.' The best part of living up here is the relaxed atmosphere. People up here are great."

A traveler will find this same friendly attitude in the city as in the country. Pittsburgh, though a thriving urban center of half a million and one of the largest hubs of research and development in the country, is really a city of small, tightly knit neighborhoods. It is also one of the safest and friendliest cities in the United States. Philadelphia, although a larger city, is still a place tourists find welcoming and like to return to time and time again.

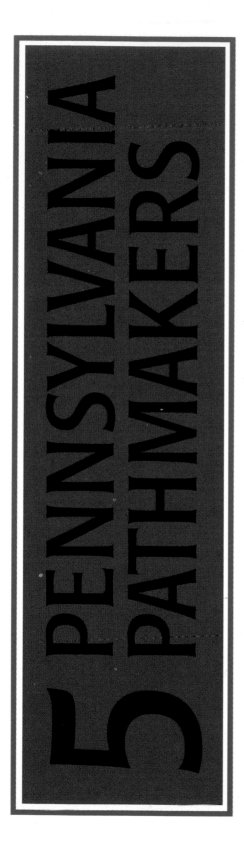

5 PENNSYLVANIA PATHMAKERS

Just as the early settlers forged a path through Pennsylvania to the West, residents and natives of the state have been pathmakers ever since. Many Pennsylvanians have made far-reaching contributions to the nation.

THE POLITICAL WORLD

Certainly Benjamin Franklin and others who signed the Declaration of Independence in 1776 were political pathmakers. But there have been many, many more.

Pathmaker Gifford Pinchot always loved wandering in the woods of his family's estate near Philadelphia and decided that he would become a professional forester. Through his forestry career he became a close adviser to President Theodore Roosevelt. Together, they enacted many reforms, including setting aside lands for protection and creating the U.S. Forest Service. Later, Pinchot served two terms as Pennsylvania's governor. But he remained first and foremost a forester all his life. "The care of the forests," he said, "is the duty of the nation."

Though pathmaker Bayard Rustin never held public office, he had a great impact on the political and social life of the nation. Born in 1912 near Philadelphia, he grew up learning Quaker values from his mother. Although Rustin attended a mostly white school, only later

Social activist Bayard Rustin is best remembered as the man who almost single-handedly organized the huge 1963 civil rights March on Washington. He spent his life fighting for civil rights and for better conditions and wages for working people.

did he feel the sting of racial discrimination. He became socially active, adopting radical views about how society needed to be changed. He helped found the Congress of Racial Equality (CORE) and was active in the Congress of Industrial Organizations (CIO) and many other organizations. CORE and the CIO did much to promote racial equality and fair treatment for working people. Bayard Rustin's greatest achievement, however, came in 1963. That year he organized the biggest civil rights demonstration in history, the March on Washington, D.C., where Dr. Martin Luther King Jr. gave his famous "I Have a Dream" speech. The march was Rustin's proudest moment.

ARTISTS

Pennsylvania has bred important artists from colonial times to the present. Benjamin West, who was born in 1738, began drawing as a young boy. His reputation spread quickly as he moved to Lancaster and then to Philadelphia to paint people's portraits. However, if you wanted to become a truly great artist then, you had to study in Europe. Because they thought West a true genius, a group of Pennsylvania art lovers raised money to send him to Europe to study.

In Rome, people flocked to see the man from wild, young America. They were less interested in his painting than in the fact that he had actually spoken with Indians! His painting improved quickly and dramatically during his stay in Italy. When he stopped in England on his way back to America in 1763, the great reaction to his work convinced him to stay. He made his career in England, winning both patronage and friendship from King George III—as well as an international reputation.

The situation for young artists in America had changed by the middle of the next century, when sixteen-year-old Mary Cassatt entered the Pennsylvania Academy of the Fine Arts in Philadelphia. Her father cared deeply about her education and wanted to see her further her artistic skills. However, Mary upset him when she announced that she intended to be a professional artist. At that

Painter Benjamin West earned an international reputation for his work. Though he sided with the American Revolution, he maintained his friendship with King George III.

Painter Mary Cassatt sat for this portrait by her friend and fellow impressionist Edgar Degas in 1884.

time, people of their class thought it good for young women to develop their artistic talent—but only as a hobby. Women were to get married and be taken care of by a man! Their artistic inclinations would make them better companions for men, perhaps better decorators of homes.

But Mary Cassatt meant what she said. She intended to be a professional painter. Her father respected her wishes and supported her. In 1866, she set out for Paris. Little by little, Cassatt made a name and a living for herself. But she soon grew bored with traditional painting styles. She admired the lively colors and everyday subjects of the painters then just beginning to make their mark. These painters, known as impressionists because they painted the eye's first, quick impression of a scene rather than the most accurate, photographic details, rejected the dark colors and realism then in fashion. Risking her career and good living, she began experimenting with impressionism. This led to a creative flowering. For the rest of her life she painted figures from everyday life, parents with children and people doing everyday things, in bright, daring colors.

Another Pennsylvania artist, Andy Warhol from Pittsburgh, helped found an artistic movement called pop art. This art takes its inspiration from popular culture—advertising, comic books, and the movies. A sickly little boy, Andy preferred staying at home reading comic books to going to school. But he showed early promise as an artist. He eventually studied design and illustration at the Carnegie Institute of Technology. After that he moved to New York to make his living as a commercial artist. He went from business to business to show his work, carrying his samples around in

Pittsburgh native Andy Warhol became famous for his flamboyant lifestyle and wit as well as his whimsical art.

a brown paper bag. After a while, he started making a lot of money doing advertising and magazine illustration. This made him happy because he had always wanted to be rich. But he also wanted to be famous as a serious artist.

Meeting this goal wasn't easy. Things didn't go well at first. But then he hit upon an idea: he would paint what we see every day but don't think about. He began painting things like Campbell's soup cans, but in his own, playful way. Finally he began to be taken seriously. He made many copies of his paintings for sale, becoming so busy that he hired his friends and mother to help him. He and his friends all worked together in a huge studio they called the Factory.

Of course, not all the great artists who came from Pennsylvania were painters. Marian Anderson of Philadelphia became an internationally known concert singer and a symbol of courage and dignity. Because she was black, she was denied the right to sing at Constitution Hall in Washington, D.C., in 1939. The owners of the building, the Daughters of the American Revolution (DAR), said they didn't want African Americans to perform there. Eleanor Roosevelt, the president's wife, resigned from the DAR and helped to arrange for a concert at the Lincoln Memorial. Marian Anderson went on to sing at New York's Metropolitan Opera, to win a Presidential Medal of Freedom, and to serve as a United States representative at the United Nations.

Philadelphia concert singer Marian Anderson, through her amazing voice, determination, and dignity, became beloved worldwide. Italian conductor Arturo Toscannini told her, "A voice like yours is heard once in a hundred years."

WRITERS

Of the many pathmaking writers who came from Pennsylvania, Elizabeth Cochran Seaman perhaps comes first. She was born in western Pennsylvania in 1864, a time when women were not expected to have careers, let alone careers that challenged how things worked. In fact, women were often prevented from having careers, and that happened at first to Elizabeth.

After Elizabeth's father died, her family fell on hard times. Elizabeth had to find work. She began writing newspaper articles, but no editor would buy them because they were written by a woman. She had to take in laundry to earn money. When she saw a nasty newspaper article making fun of women who tried to have careers, she wrote an angry letter to the editor. The editor liked the letter so much that he invited Elizabeth to come to his office and talk. He then offered her a job. Her first article, "Mad Marriage," argued that women should be allowed to divorce abusive husbands and that they shouldn't be forced into marriages they didn't want, a daring position to take at the time. Her editor suggested that Elizabeth use a pen name to protect herself and her family. She chose the name Nellie Bly, from a popular song.

Nellie Bly became the first woman undercover investigative reporter. She wrote stories about the mistreatment of workers in sweatshops, where workers were locked into unsafe, hot factories for long hours without so much as a bathroom break. She also wrote about inhumane conditions in prisons and in mental hospitals. Each time, she had to pretend to be someone else and actually go into these dangerous situations and gather firsthand information.

Elizabeth Cochran Seaman, better known as Nellie Bly, completed her trip around the world in a record seventy-two days, six hours, and eleven minutes. She probably did her most lasting work, however, on behalf of people being mistreated at work and in hospitals for the mentally ill.

Her articles and books led to laws that helped improve conditions. But her greatest fame came in the winter of 1889–1890, when she traveled around the world in a race to beat the record set by writer

Jules Verne's fictional character Phileas Fogg in *Around the World in Eighty Days*. Attracting international attention, Nellie Bly traveled around the world in seventy-two days!

SHOW BUSINESS

If you have ever watched the movie *It's a Wonderful Life* at Christmastime, you have seen James Stewart. He plays small-town banker George Bailey, who is helped through hard times by an angel

This scene from the 1946 movie It's a Wonderful Life, *about a small-town banker facing a terrible crisis in his life, could have taken place in the town where star James Stewart (right) grew up, Indiana, Pennsylvania.*

named Clarence. Maybe Stewart played this part so well because he came from a small town and lived many of the values in the movie.

James Stewart grew up in Indiana, Pennsylvania. As a boy, he learned to play the accordion from an Italian barber and played each week on the town hall steps with the Boy Scout band. He also hurdled and high jumped in school, worked on the yearbook, and sang in the choir. In 1935, he traveled to Hollywood to begin his movie career. He soon became one of the biggest stars in Hollywood. During World War II, when many other actors stayed home and made training films or played soldiers in movies, James Stewart put on the uniform for real. As a pilot, he flew twenty combat missions over Europe, earning the Distinguished Flying Cross, the Air Medal, and seven Battle Stars.

Another Hollywood success story, Grace Kelly, came from a well-to-do Philadelphia family and began her acting career in New York. After graduating from New York's American Academy of Dramatic Arts, she became an instant success. When she was only twenty-two, she played a Quaker wife who wants her husband to give up gunfighting in the movie *High Noon*. She starred in many movies, and in one, *Rear Window*, she played alongside James Stewart. In 1954, she won an Oscar for her role in *The Country Girl*.

At the height of her stardom, she fell in love with Prince Rainier of Monaco. Reporters and fans followed the couple everywhere and wanted to know everything about them. In 1955, they were married. After her marriage, the new Princess Grace devoted her time and energy for the rest of her life to charitable works.

Another Philadelphian, Bill Cosby, began his career early, as the class clown cracking up his schoolmates. After many years of enter-

Actress Grace Kelly gave up a brilliant career in the movies to marry Prince Rainier of Monaco. Here she is seen shortly before becoming Princess Grace.

taining friends and coworkers with funny stories, Cosby found himself onstage telling jokes and stories. Within a few years, he was appearing on talk shows, making record albums, and playing the biggest stages in the country.

In 1965, Cosby became the first African American to play a serious leading role on a television series when he starred in *I Spy*. Since then he has appeared in a number of television series. His

Philadelphia-born-and-raised Bill Cosby started out as a funny man in clubs and has grown into a television star and role model for fathers.

award-winning *The Cosby Show* illustrated for many men how to be a caring and firm but funny father.

INDUSTRIALISTS

Two of Pennsylvania's biggest industrialists gave much of their fortune away.

Scottish-born Andrew Carnegie came to Pennsylvania a poor boy in 1848. He started out working in a Pittsburgh cotton mill at thirteen. Soon afterward, he took a job delivering telegraph messages around the city. In his free time, Andrew taught himself Morse code, which was how telegrams were sent. After learning this skill, he was promoted to telegraph operator. Then he became the

MISTER ROGERS

"I like you just the way you are."

You probably remember hearing Mister Rogers say those words, but do you know where he first heard them? He heard them from his grandfather when he was little, and he never forgot them. They made a huge difference in his life.

Fred Rogers grew up in Latrobe, Pennsylvania, and began his television career in nearby Pittsburgh in the mid-1950s. He never planned to be on television. Instead, he thought he would be a musician or a minister. In fact, he started college as a music composition major. After graduation, he took a job with a television station in New York. He felt television had a lot of positive potential that was being wasted. Within a couple of years, he was working at the country's first community-supported television station in Pittsburgh. Then, while writing and producing a program called *The Children's Corner*, he enrolled in Pittsburgh Theological Seminary and was ordained a Presbyterian minister in 1963.

Mr. Rogers has been making up songs and stories for children ever since. Through his show, *Mr. Rogers' Neighborhood*, children are his congregation.

assistant to the superintendent of the railroad company in western Pennsylvania—and then superintendent!

Each new job brought higher pay, and Carnegie saved and invested the money. He invested in railroad sleeping cars because he knew people would need to be comfortable as they traveled long distances across the country. He invested in iron bridges because the wooden ones used at that time sometimes burned or collapsed. He invested in oil and coal. During the Civil War, he helped the

Self-made man Andrew Carnegie built the steel mills that built Pittsburgh, then dedicated his fortune to philanthropy. "He who dies rich," said Carnegie, "dies disgraced."

Union army repair railway tracks and telegraph lines. By 1865, he had made enough from his investments to quit his job and go to work for himself. He saw a future in steel because it was stronger than iron, and by 1890 he had made Pittsburgh the largest steel producer in the country.

In 1901, Carnegie sold his empire for $250 million. He spent the rest of his life donating his money to good causes. He paid for more than two thousand libraries and eight thousand church organs in Great Britain, Canada, and the United States.

Candy maker Milton S. Hershey also started poor. He grew up in the country east of Harrisburg. After a series of business failures, he finally made his first million by selling caramel to a company in England. His real breakthrough came, however, when he discovered that the English company had covered his caramel in chocolate. At a party, he noticed English children licking the chocolate off his candy and throwing the caramel away. From this hint of what children liked, he developed Hershey's Milk Chocolate Bar in 1900. Then, in 1907, he invented Hershey's Kisses.

He made so much money that he started his own town near his home. The town included a community center, a department store, a movie theater, an amusement park and zoo, and houses for his workers. In 1909, Hershey and his wife founded Hershey Industrial School for orphaned boys. In his school, boys were educated and taught a trade. Later it was renamed Milton Hershey School, the curriculum was expanded, and girls were admitted. Today, not all the students are orphaned, though they do all come from poor families. Students at Milton Hershey School receive all their clothing, medical expenses, and education completely free of charge. Today, the majority of the stock in Hershey Foods is owned by the school.

SPORTS FIGURES

Penn State football coach Joe Paterno is a hero because he has led the Nittany Lions to national championships, but he is also a hero for other reasons. Throughout his long career, Paterno has spoken out for high academic standards. He has won the respect of many people who don't even like football because he insists that

Here Wilt "the Stilt" Chamberlain, number 13, shoots the ball over his opponent's head, as he did so successfully for so long.

his players excel in the classroom as well as on the field.

Wilt Chamberlain, one of the greatest basketball players ever, began playing professionally in 1958 for the Harlem Globetrotters. The very next year, however, he moved back to his hometown of Philadelphia to play for the Warriors and then for the 76ers. Just over seven feet tall, Chamberlain earned the nickname Wilt the Stilt. He scored a record one hundred points in a 1962 game. Even after he went on to play for the Los Angeles Lakers, Philadelphians still took pride in him.

6 "MEMORIES LAST A LIFETIME"

First-time visitors to Pennsylvania often think they already know what they are going to see. Some think they will see only cities and factories. Others think they will see only Amish farms and horses and buggies. They'll see all of that, of course. But they will see much more, too. Pennsylvania offers the kind of experiences people never forget. As the Pennsylvania Department of Tourism says, "Memories Last a Lifetime." Let's take a quick drive through the state and find out more of what there is to see and do.

AROUND PHILADELPHIA

We'll begin where Pennsylvania began—in Philadelphia. The locals call it Philly.

Independence National Historical Park is a good place to start. At Independence Hall guides will tell you about the drafting of the Declaration of Independence and other historic events that took place there. At the Liberty Bell Pavilion you may be surprised to learn that the Liberty Bell didn't crack on July 4, 1776. Rather, it cracked the very first time it rang in 1752. Recast twice, it then cracked in 1835, when it rang for thirty-six hours after Chief Justice of the Supreme Court John Marshall died and again in 1846 when it rang for George Washington's birthday.

Another way to explore Philly is by visiting the city's excellent

Fourth of July fireworks light up Independence Hall in Philadelphia and provide a fitting spectacle at the nation's birthplace.

museums. For example, if you can't be in town on New Year's Day, when the uniquely Philadelphian Mummers hold their annual parade of string bands, fancy-dress brigades, grown men driving go-carts, and cavorting clowns, you might want to visit their

PLACES TO SEE

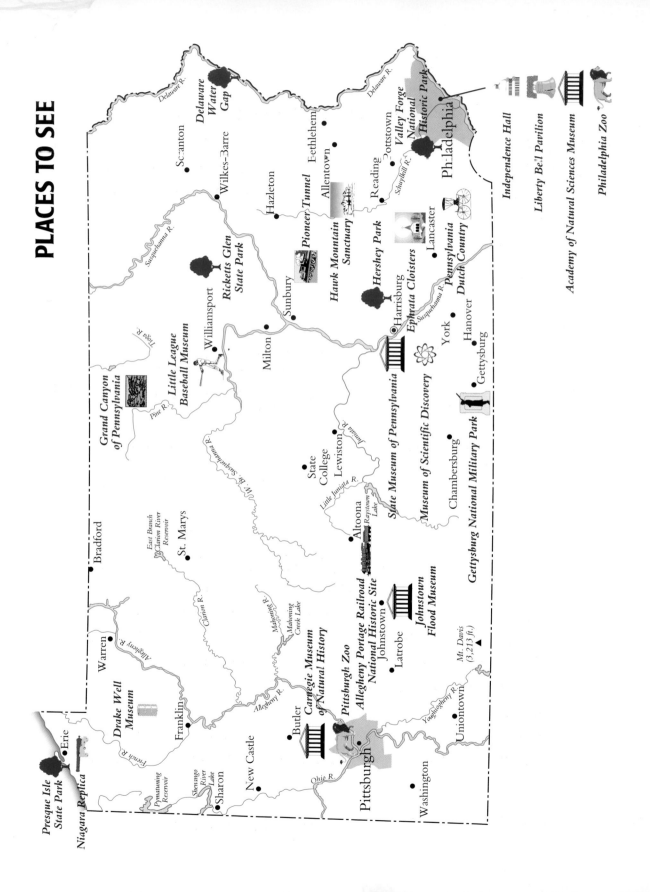

Presque Isle State Park

Niagara Replica

Drake Well Museum

Grand Canyon of Pennsylvania

Little League Baseball Museum

Ricketts Glen State Park

Delaware Water Gap

Pioneer Tunnel

Hawk Mountain Sanctuary

Hershey Park

Ephrata Cloisters

Pennsylvania Dutch Country

State Museum of Pennsylvania

Museum of Scientific Discovery

Gettysburg National Military Park

Allegheny Portage Railroad National Historic Site

Johnstown Flood Museum

Carnegie Museum of Natural History

Pittsburgh Zoo

Independence Hall

Liberty Bell Pavilion

Academy of Natural Sciences Museum

Philadelphia Zoo

Erie

Bradford

Warren

Franklin

New Castle

Sharon

St. Marys

Williamsport

Scranton

Wilkes-Barre

Hazleton

Bethlehem

Allentown

Reading

Pottstown

Philadelphia

Sunbury

Milton

State College

Lewiston

Altoona

Harrisburg

Lancaster

York

Hanover

Gettysburg

Chambersburg

Johnstown

Latrobe

Butler

Pittsburgh

Washington

Uniontown

Mt. Davis (3,213 ft.)

Delaware R.

Delaware R.

Susquehanna R.

Schuylkill R.

Tioga R.

Pine R.

W. Br. Susquehanna R.

Susquehanna R.

Juniata R.

Little Juniata R.

Raystown Lake

East Branch Clarion River Reservoir

Clarion R.

Mahoning R.

Mahoning Creek Lake

Allegheny R.

Allegheny R.

French R.

Shenango River Lake

Pymatuning Reservoir

Ohio R.

Youghiogheny R.

TEN LARGEST CITIES

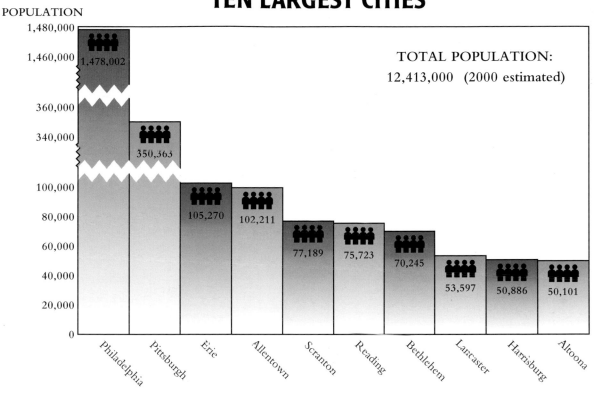

POPULATION

TOTAL POPULATION:
12,413,000   (2000 estimated)

1,480,000
1,460,000 — 1,478,002 — Philadelphia
360,000
340,000 — 350,363 — Pittsburgh
100,000 — 105,270 — Erie
80,000 — 102,211 — Allentown
60,000 — 77,189 — Scranton
— 75,723 — Reading
— 70,245 — Bethlehem
40,000 — 53,597 — Lancaster
— 50,886 — Harrisburg
20,000 — 50,101 — Altoona
0

museum. There you can view displays of the crazy outfits the Mummers, an organization of New Year's clubs that dates back to the 1840s, have worn through the years. If you're into science, try the Academy of Natural Sciences Museum, founded in 1812. One of their recent shows featured a fully animated dinosaur. If you like that, you'll probably also enjoy the Philadelphia Zoo, one of the oldest and best in the country.

You'll have to eat in Philly, so try the famous Philadelphia cheesesteak (delicious!). One Philadelphian transplanted to

Minnesota actually had one of these steak, onion, and melted cheese sandwiches airfreighted across the country, she missed it so much! "They always taste better when they are straight from Philly," she said. You might also try one of those huge, hot Philly pretzels (with lots of mustard), or go food shopping in the Italian street market that started about the time of the Civil War. This is more than shopping. It's an adventure for all five senses.

North of Philly, at Valley Forge National Historical Park, you can visit the house where George Washington spent the winter and see

One way to fall in love with history is to visit Valley Forge and imagine what it must have been like that terrible winter of 1777–1778.

re-creations of the cabins his soldiers built. Farther north, in Bucks County, are some simple stone Quaker meetinghouses built in the 1680s. In New Hope you can ride a mule-drawn barge on the Delaware Canal.

POCONO MOUNTAINS REGION

Do you like to ski? Well, if you keep driving north, you reach the Pocono Mountains, with its beautiful views and excellent ski slopes. Thirteen top-rated ski resorts and many state parks give outdoors enthusiasts plenty of options. At Ricketts Glen State Park you can hike to twenty-two waterfalls, the highest being the ninety-four-foot Ganoga Falls. Then there is the gorgeous Delaware Water Gap, where the Delaware River cuts through the mountains. This region is a favorite during fall, when the leaves turn spectacular colors.

For those interested in history, Ashland is the place to be. At the Pioneer Tunnel, you can ride a narrow gauge train 1,800 feet into a coal mine that closed in 1935. Your guide will explain how miners dug coal and hauled it to the surface using mules.

Not far away is Hawk Mountain Sanctuary, a favorite of bird-watchers and hikers. Although the hiking trails are always spectacular, Hawk Mountain is an especially exciting place to be from September through November, when more than 24,000 raptors—birds of prey—fly over the area.

CENTRAL PENNSYLVANIA

Driving west, we enter central Pennsylvania, an area of gentle

The Delaware Water Gap provides an awesome setting for canoeing and other outdoor activities.

beauty and wonderful surprises. Williamsport, along the Susquehanna River, is the birthplace of Little League baseball and the site of the annual Little League Baseball World Series. At the Little League Baseball Museum, you can watch video highlights of past games and test your own skills in the bat and pitch cages. You can even see how well you did on video replays of yourself.

Farther west, stop in Bellefonte, a once rich industrial town. The downtown, with its classic courthouse and square, evokes a slower time. As you walk through this hilly town of restored mansions with turrets (like towers) and fanciful, old-fashioned designs, you begin to get an idea of what a rich nineteenth-century American town was like. Just down the road is the Mid-State Trail, which follows Tussey Mountain overlooking Penns Valley. In Bald Eagle Valley, you can ride a glider, soaring quietly over the ridges on the same drafts of air eagles ride.

Young players from Japan and America greet each other at the Little League World Series in Williamsport.

HEADING NORTH

Driving north, we have gotten about as far from city life as we can go. "We are so far removed from the rest of the state," says Tioga County historian Scott Gitchell, "it's hard to see how other things in the state affect us. Unless it's a really controversial issue, people up here don't pay a lot of attention. We're more interested in remembering our pioneer past."

Going west, you can start to feel that past. At the Grand Canyon of Pennsylvania, you can stand next to the fifty-mile-long, one thousand-foot-deep drop into Pine Creek Gorge. If you want, you can raft down the creek. Eugenia Keeney runs one of the many rafting rentals. But she'll do more than rent you a raft; she'll also teach you local history. "I was born and raised here all my life," she grins happily. "The King of the Canyon, Ed McCarthy, started doing this back in the 1950s with army surplus rafts. . . . He said his son and I lost our baby bottles floating down the creek. We grew up on the creek. I wouldn't live anywhere else."

Farther west is the Allegheny National Forest, Pennsylvania's only national forest. This is a great place for camping, hiking, biking, canoeing, or just driving scenic back roads. Many trails have been designated for cross-country skiing or snowmobiling. It is also the site of one of Pennsylvania's few old-growth forest stands, Tionesta Scenic Region, a truly magical place.

Nearby, you can explore the early history of oil drilling by visiting the Drake Well Museum in Titusville or Oil Creek State Park. The park is seven thousand acres of trails that take you through ghost towns, cemeteries, and abandoned wells. The excursion train of the

Oil Creek and Titusville Railroad is a fun way to see this area.

To the northwest are the shores of Lake Erie and Pennsylvania's third-largest city, Erie. There you can view a re-creation of the ship *Niagara*, commanded by Commodore Oliver Perry when he defeated the British fleet in the War of 1812. Erie is also the home of Waldameer Park and Water World, two amusement parks featuring a host of thrill rides and water slides.

Beautiful beaches line Lake Erie. If you want to hike and enjoy the natural scenery, Presque Isle State Park and the Erie National Wildlife Refuge are great spots.

The shores of Lake Erie offer fine beaches for swimming or just getting your feet wet.

PITTSBURGH

Driving south through the rolling countryside of western Pennsylvania, you will reach Pittsburgh, where big city life begins once again. Of the many sights in Pittsburgh, two are musts: the Carnegie Museum of Natural History and the Pittsburgh Zoo. At the natural history museum, you'll see gemstones, dinosaur skeletons, and exhibits of endangered plants and animals. You can also ride an imaginary elevator deep into the earth to view the layers of rock underneath Pennsylvania's surface. At the zoo, you can climb a giant rope spiderweb or experience life in the treetops at the Canopy Walk. Other exhibits take you right into animal habitats under the ground or water.

THE SOUTHERN ALLEGHENIES

There is much to see of history, nature, and industry driving east from Pittsburgh. For those interested in history, reenactors put on a good show of a French and Indian War battle at Fort Ligonier and a great depiction of early American life at Old Bedford Village. Some of the best skiing in the state is done at Blue Knob Ski Resort. And at Ohiopyle, the Youghiogheny (yock-a-GAY-nee) River cuts through the Laurel Ridge, creating a 1,700-foot-deep gorge popular with rafters.

Today, the southern Alleghenies' contribution to the industrial development of Pennsylvania is commemorated in the Path of Progress. Trails, parks, and heritage sites mark the five-hundred-mile route. At the Allegheny Portage Railroad National Historic Site

Old Bedford Village takes visitors back to pioneer days. Historical reenactors demonstrate colonial skills like hearth cooking, blacksmithing, spinning, weaving, and quilt making.

atop Cresson Mountain, see models of the pulley system that carried people and canal boats across the Allegheny Front. Visit the 160-year-old Lemon House, the tavern where travelers stopped and ate during their crossing. Then go to see the Horseshoe Curve National Historic Landmark nearby. This curved track carries trains eighty-five feet higher each mile. Like the portage, it's an amazing feat of engineering.

THE JOHNSTOWN FLOOD

On May 31, 1889, the worst peacetime disaster in the nation's history took place when the South Fork Dam, sixteen miles upstream from Johnstown, broke. It sent a roaring forty-foot wall of water rushing down upon the city. Everything in its path was destroyed. When the waters subsided a tremendous fire broke out, which added to the misery and destruction. The flood left 35,000 people homeless and 2,200 dead.

On a bal - my day in May, When na - ture held full sway, And the birds sang sweet - ly in the sky a - bove. A ci - ty lay se - rene in a val - ley deep and green, Where thou - sands dwelt in hap - pi - ness and love.

Chorus
Now, the cry of dis - tress from the east to the west, And our whole dear coun - try now is plunged in woe.

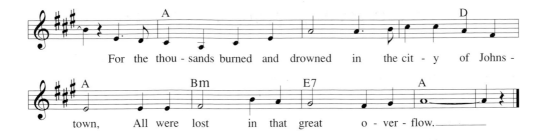

For the thou - sands burned and drowned in the cit - y of Johns - town, All were lost in that great o - ver - flow._____

Like the Paul Revere of old,
Came a rider brave and bold;
On a big horse he was flying like a deer.
And he shouted warning shrill,
"Quickly fly off to the hills."
But the people smiled and showed no sign of fear. *Chorus*

Ah! but e'er he turned away,
This brave rider and the bay,
From the many thousand souls he tried to save,
Than they had no time to spare,
Nor to offer up a prayer.
For they were swept off to a watery grave. *Chorus*

Fathers, mothers, children, all,
Both the young, old, great and small,
They were thrown about like chaff before the wind;
When the fearful raging flood,
Rushing where the city stood,
Leaving thousands dead and dying there behind. *Chorus*

Now the cry of fire arose,
Like the scream of battling foes,
For that dreadful sick'ning pile was now on fire.
As they poured out prayers to heaven,
They were burned as in an oven,
And that dreadful ruin formed their funeral pyre. *Chorus*

Not to be missed along the Path of Progress is the Johnstown Flood Museum. In 1889, a neglected dam burst during a heavy rainfall. The forty-foot wave that crashed down the valley of the Little Conemaugh picked up everything in its path. The wave smashed into Johnstown, killing more than two thousand people and destroying the town. The museum documents the flood with exhibits and an Academy Award–winning film.

THE DUTCH COUNTRY

Driving east across the southern Alleghenies, we reach the beautifully preserved Gettysburg Battlefield. Climb through the rocks of Little Round Top, the scene of fierce fighting. Walk across the open fields of Pickett's Charge. Local stables rent horses you can ride over large parts of the battlefield. You can also hire a guide to go over the battlefield with you to tell the stories you might otherwise never learn.

Driving north from Gettysburg, we reach the state capital, Harrisburg. Like many of Pennsylvania's smaller cities, it's a pretty place with row houses and shaded streets. Spend time at the State Museum of Pennsylvania, which shows you Pennsylvania 3.6 billion years ago. Then walk up the street to the Museum of Scientific Discovery, where computers bring science to life.

Driving east from Harrisburg, you enter the Dutch Country, one of the state's major tourist attractions. Here are miles of tidy Amish and Mennonite farms. Drive slowly on the back roads, because you might run into a horse and buggy if you're not careful. It is also good to remember that the Amish are serious people living their

BRINGING THE CIVIL WAR TO LIFE

If you go to Gettysburg in July, you may see serious Civil War buffs reenact the battle. In 1998, more than 35,000 people dressed in the uniforms of the North and South for the event.

Jo An Yoder and her husband and son, who live in Lancaster, spend many of their free weekends taking part in Civil War reenactments. Her husband and son dress in Union artillery regiment uniforms, while Jo An dresses as a wife visiting from home. "The wives used to come to the camps and they would dress pretty to sort of cheer their husbands up," says Jo An. "Like today, I'm wearing the colors of the regiment in my dress. That's what some of the women would do."

Civil War reenactors work hard to make their clothing and equipment as much like it would have been in the 1860s as possible. Jo An and her friends enjoy creating their costumes and uniforms. "I make hats and parasols for some of the other women. Then some of them make dresses or shawls or uniform shirts, and we trade. We help each other out."

This is a way for Jo An and her family to socialize during their vacations. "We do reenactments all over and have developed a lot of friendships with other people who do this."

The Amish refer to their English-speaking neighbors as "English."
Here an Amish farmer gives his "English" neighbor a ride in his
pony cart as an Amish boy tends a roadside vegetable stand.

In Hershey, the town that chocolate built, the whole family can camp,
tour the factory, golf, or visit HersheyPark, seen here decked out for
Christmas.

lives according to their religious beliefs. It is not polite to take pictures of them unless you first ask permission. For some, this may be a serious religious matter. Respect their customs.

Another popular attraction is Hershey, chocolate-maker Milton Hershey's town. At Hershey's Chocolate World Visitor's Center, you can ride a railcar on a chocolate-making tour and get free samples at the end. After that, head for the rides at HersheyPark or watch the animals at ZooAmerica. Indian Echo Caverns is

CELEBRATING DUTCHINESS

Pennsylvanians of German ancestry take great pride in being Pennsylvania Dutch. After all, when most people think of Pennsylvania, they think of Amish farms, shoofly pie, and funny Dutchified sayings such as "The hurrier I go, the behinder I get." So it is only natural that they celebrate their unique culture.

For decades visitors have been dipping into their culture at the annual Kutztown Pennsylvania Dutch Folk Festival. It's a celebration of "Dutchiness" then and now.

Craftspeople demonstrate quilt making, blacksmithing, weaving, and other skills. Expert marksmen demonstrate firing the Pennsylvania long rifle, which later became known as the Kentucky rifle. Old time Dutchy comedians entertain, polka bands play, and kids enjoy themselves at a hay maze and petting zoo.

"Komm rei, huck dich un essa," say the posters for this get-together. "Come in, sit down, and eat!"

Indeed, that's the way it works: there is always plenty to do and always plenty of delicious food to eat.

nearby. There you walk through rooms of magical rock formations with names like the Diamond Fairyland and hear about William Wilson, who lived in the caves for nineteen years.

Drive farther east to visit historic Ephrata Cloisters, one of the more unusual communities in Penn's Holy Experiment. The members of the community believed that one grew closer to God by withdrawing from the world. Each "brother" and "sister," as they were called, slept in a tiny "cell," using a block of wood, believe it or not, as a pillow. Strict vegetarians, they ate their first simple meal of the day at 5 A.M. They were also great lovers of music and composed more than a thousand hymns and chorales. Today the brothers and sisters are all gone, but the historic buildings are well kept and worth touring. In 1777, General George Washington ordered that soldiers wounded at the Battle of Brandywine be taken there for care. One soldier later wrote, "I came upon these people by accident; I leave with regret."

In fact, that is the way you may feel at the end of your tour of Pennsylvania, where memories do last a lifetime.

THE FLAG: The state flag consists of the state coat of arms between two horses against a blue background. The coat of arms includes a ship, a plow, and wheat, which represent commerce and agriculture. Above is an eagle, symbolizing bravery. The olive branch below represents peace, and the cornstalk, prosperity. The flag was adopted in 1907.

THE SEAL: The state seal, which was adopted in 1791, includes a version of the state coat of arms against a white background.

STATE SURVEY

Statehood: December 12, 1787

Origin of Name: Pennsylvania means "Penn's woods" in Latin. It was named in honor of William Penn, the father of Pennsylvania's founder.

Nickname: Keystone State

Capital: Harrisburg

Motto: Virtue, Liberty, and Independence

Bird: Ruffed grouse

Flower: Mountain laurel

Tree: Hemlock

Animal: White-tailed deer

Dog: Great Dane

Ruffed grouse

Mountain laurel

PENNSYLVANIA

The official state song of the Commonwealth of Pennsylvania was adopted by the general assembly and signed into law by Governor Robert P. Casey on November 29, 1990.

Words and Music by
Eddie Khoury and Ronnie Bonner

Fish: Brook trout

Insect: Firefly

Beverage: Milk

Fossil: Phacops rana

GEOGRAPHY

Highest Point: 3,213 feet above sea level, at Mount Davis

Lowest Point: sea level along the Delaware River

Area: 45,310 square miles

Greatest Distance, North to South: 175 miles

Greatest Distance, East to West: 306 miles

Bordering States: New York to the north, New Jersey to the east, Maryland and Delaware to the south, West Virginia to the south and west, Ohio to the west

Hottest Recorded Temperature: 111°F in Phoenixville on July 10, 1936

Coldest Recorded Temperature: -42°F in Smethport on January 5, 1904

Average Annual Precipitation: 41 inches

Major Rivers: Allegheny, Beaver, Conemaugh, Delaware, Juniata, Lehigh, Monongahela, Ohio, Schuylkill, Susquehanna, Youghiogheny

Major Lakes: Arthur, Conneaut, Erie, Pymatuning, Raystown

Trees: ash, aspen, basswood, beech, birch, black cherry, hemlock, hickory, maple, oak, pine, sycamore, walnut

Wild Plants: azalea, blackberry, bloodroot, bouncing Bet, dogwood, fern, hepatica, honeysuckle, milkweed, raspberry, rhododendron, sundew, wintergreen

Animals: beaver, black bear, deer, mink, muskrat, rabbit, raccoon, squirrel, skunk, timber rattlesnake, turtle

Beaver

Birds: barn swallow, bobwhite quail, Canada goose, duck, nuthatch, osprey, owl, partridge, pine grosbeak, ring-necked pheasant, wild turkey

Fish: bass, brown trout, carp, catfish, chub, muskellunge, northern pike, pickerel, walleye

Endangered Animals: American peregrine falcon, clubshell, cracking pearly-mussel, dwarf wedgemussel, Indiana bat, northern riffleshell, orangefoot pimpleback, pink mucket, piping plover, ring pink, rough pigtoe

Endangered Plants: northeastern bulrush

American peregrine falcon

TIMELINE

Pennsylvania History

1500s The Leni-Lenape, Erie, Naticoke, Shawnee, and Susquehannock Indians live in present-day Pennsylvania

1615 Dutch explorer Cornelius Hendricksen sails up the Delaware River to the site of present-day Philadelphia

1638 New Sweden, the first European settlement in present-day Pennsylvania, is established near Philadelphia

1643 The Dutch found Pennsylvania's first permanent European settlement on Tinicum Island

1664 The English gain control of the Pennsylvania region

1681 King Charles II of England grants Pennsylvania to William Penn

1719 Pennsylvania's first newspaper, the *American Weekly Mercury*, begins publication in Philadelphia

1731 The first circulating library in the American colonies opens in Philadelphia

1754 The French and Indian War begins in western Pennsylvania

1767 Charles Mason and Jeremiah Dixon complete their survey of the Pennsylvania-Maryland border, creating the Mason-Dixon Line between the North and the South

1776 The Declaration of Independence is signed in Philadelphia

1777 General George Washington and his troops settle in for a brutal winter at Valley Forge during the Revolutionary War

1784 The *Pennsylvania Packet and General Advertiser* becomes the nation's first daily newspaper

1787 The U.S. Constitution is drawn up in Philadelphia; Pennsylvania becomes the second state

1791 Philadelphia carpenters walk off the job to demand a 12-hour work-day in the nation's first strike

1794 The country's first major hard-surfaced road opens between Philadelphia and Lancaster

1812 Harrisburg becomes the state capital

1825 The Schuylkill Canal opens, connecting Philadelphia and Reading

1859 The nation's first commercially successful oil well is drilled near Titusville

1861–1865 About 340,000 Pennsylvanians join the Union army during the Civil War

1863 Union troops win the Battle of Gettysburg

1889 More than 2,000 people die in the Johnstown flood

1892 Violence erupts during a strike at the Homestead steel plant

1917 The United States enters World War I

1920 KDKA in Pittsburgh, the nation's first commercial radio station, begins broadcasting

1940 The first section of the Pennsylvania Turnpike opens

1941 The United States enters World War II

1971 The state legislature establishes an individual income tax and a state lottery

1979 The worst nuclear accident in U.S. history occurs at the Three Mile Island power plant near Harrisburg

1985 A group of tornadoes strike Pennsylvania, killing 65 people

ECONOMY

Agricultural Products: apples, beef cattle, corn, eggs, greenhouse and nursery products, hay, hogs, milk, mushrooms, oats, potatoes, poultry

Mushrooms

Manufactured Products: chemicals, clothing, electrical equipment, food products, glass products, machinery, printed materials, steel, transportation equipment

Natural Resources: coal, iron, limestone, natural gas, oil, sand and gravel

Business and Trade: banking, health care, tourism, wholesale and retail trade

CALENDAR OF CELEBRATIONS

Mummer's Parade Philadelphia welcomes the New Year with its silliest parade, featuring banjo players, outrageous costumes, and go-carts.

Groundhog Day Each February 2, the eyes of the nation turn to the small town of Punxsatawney to witness the weather prediction made by a groundhog named Punxsatawney Phil. If he sees his shadow when he leaves his burrow, it means six more weeks of winter. No shadow is a sign of an early spring.

National Ice-Carving Championship Competitors bring their blowtorches, chainsaws, and chisels to create wondrous sculptures at this February contest in Scranton.

Valborgsmassoafton Welcome spring in the traditional Swedish way at this joyous festival in Philadelphia, which features lots of singing, dancing, great food, and a spectacular bonfire.

Devon Horse Show and County Fair Each May in Devon, more than a thousand graceful horses compete in traditional events at America's oldest outdoor equestrian show.

Devon Horse Show and County Fair

Kutztown Pennsylvania German Festival Everyone snacks on rich, delicious funnel cake at this celebration of Pennsylvania Dutch culture in Kutztown in late June and early July. Other favorites include pretzels, shoofly pie, and dumplings. Besides eating all the food, you can enjoy folk art displays, traditional music, and a reenactment of an Amish wedding.

Fourth of July Celebrate the birth of the nation in the city where the

Declaration of Independence was signed. Each July, Philadelphia pulls out all the stops for more than a week's worth of parades, fireworks displays, concerts, sporting events, and as much food as you could possibly want.

Three Rivers Regatta Each July hundreds of boats take to the water where the Monongahela, Allegheny, and Ohio Rivers meet in Pittsburgh. The event also features water shows and boat races.

HarborFest Harborcreek honors its place on Lake Erie each July with a festival that includes skydiving exhibitions, hot air balloons, and lots of music.

Pennsylvania State Flaming Foliage Festival The tiny town of Renovo celebrates the brilliant colors of its trees each October with a parade, a crafts fair, and lots of leaf-peeping.

Bethlehem Christmas Guides in colonial costume take visitors on tours of Bethlehem's beautiful historic district during the Christmas season. You can also get into the holiday spirit with a candlelight concert or a ride in a horse-drawn carriage.

Washington Crossing the Delaware Each Christmas at Washington Crossing Historical Park in Bucks County, history buffs gather to reenact Washington and his troops crossing the Delaware River on their way to a decisive victory at the Battle of Trenton.

STATE STARS

Marian Anderson (1897–1993) possessed one of the greatest voices of the 20th century. She began singing in church choirs as a young girl and eventually trained as an opera singer. She first gained attention in 1925, when her prize for winning a singing competition was to perform with the New York Philharmonic. Anderson soon became highly regarded throughout Europe. In 1955, she became the first African American to sing at New York's Metropolitan Opera House. Anderson was born in Philadelphia.

Guion Bluford Jr. (1942–   ), an astronaut, was the first African American in space. Bluford was born in Philadelphia and attended Pennsylvania State University. He made the first of his four trips into space in 1983.

Guion Bluford Jr.

Nellie Bly (1864–1922) was a journalist famous for going undercover to expose corruption and abuse. She once spent ten days in a mental hospital to gather firsthand information about how the inmates were treated. In 1890, she made worldwide headlines when she completed a round-the-world trip in less time than it had taken the character Phileas Fogg in the novel *Around the World in Eighty Days*. Bly made it in just 72 days. Bly was born Elizabeth Cochran Seaman in Cochran's Mill.

Ed Bradley (1941–   ), a prominent broadcast journalist, was born in Philadelphia and attended college in Cheyney. Bradley first gained attention as a reporter for CBS television, covering the Vietnam War. He was eventually wounded by mortar fire. In 1976, he began hosting the *CBS Sunday Night News*, becoming the only black network anchor at the time. A few years later, Bradley became a featured reporter on the acclaimed series *60 Minutes*. He has won many awards, including several Emmys and the Overseas Press Club's Edward R. Murrow Award.

Alexander Calder (1898–1976), a sculptor born in Philadelphia, is best remembered for his whimsical mobiles. He first gained fame in the late 1920s for making portraits out of wire. Later, his art became more abstract. Today, his large, graceful mobiles can be found in public buildings and museums around the world.

Andrew Carnegie (1835–1919) made a fortune in steel production and other industries. By the turn of the century, Carnegie controlled about one-quarter of American iron and steel production and was perhaps the richest man in the world. In 1901, Carnegie sold his company and retired. Today, Carnegie is remembered for his philanthropy. He donated $350 million to various causes, endowing 2,000 libraries around the world, along with many colleges and foundations. Carnegie was born in Scotland and moved to Allegheny, Pennsylvania, as a child.

Rachel Carson (1907–1964), a marine biologist, was born in Springdale. Carson spent much of her career working for the U.S. Fish and Wildlife Service. She earned acclaim for her ability to write about science in elegant language in such books as *The Sea around Us*, which won the National Book Award in 1952. Carson is best known for *Silent Spring*, which warned the nation about the danger of pesticides and led to the banning of a pesticide called DDT.

Rachel Carson

Mary Cassatt (1844–1926), a painter, was born in Allegheny and studied at the Pennsylvania Academy of the Fine Arts in Philadelphia. In 1866, she moved to France, where she fell in with the impressionists, who painted the effect of light on objects. In her paintings, Cassatt emphasized graceful lines and natural poses and often painted intimate scenes of mothers with their children. Her most famous works include *The Boating Party* from 1883, which hangs in the National Gallery in Washington, D.C.

Wilt Chamberlain (1936–1999), one of the greatest basketball players of all time, was born in Philadelphia. The seven-foot-one-inch center, known as Wilt the Stilt, was the leading scorer in the National Basketball Association (NBA) for seven straight years in the early 1960s and is the second all-time leading scorer in NBA history. His most phenomenal year was 1962, when he averaged 50 points per game for the entire season and scored a record 100 points in one game. Chamberlain was elected to the Basketball Hall of Fame in 1978.

Bill Cosby (1937–   ), a popular actor and comedian, was born in Philadelphia. In the 1960s, Cosby played a secret agent in *I Spy*, becoming the first African American to star in a prime-time drama on television. His performances earned him the Best Actor Emmy three years in a row. Cosby reached the peak of his popularity in the late 1980s on *The Cosby Show*, playing a warm and funny father of five. He has also written many popular books, including *Fatherhood* and *Time Flies*.

Stuart Davis (1894–1964) was an influential abstract painter. His most famous paintings incorporate bright colors and lively action, taking their inspiration from jazz music. Davis was also one of the first painters to use everyday objects such as billboards and street signs in his compositions. He was born in Philadelphia.

W. C. Fields (1879–1946), a comic actor from Philadelphia, was famous for creating grumpy, sharp-tongued characters who hate children, animals, and the police. Fields entered show business at age 14. Early on, he worked in vaudeville as a comic juggler. He eventually began performing on the New York stage and then starred in such films as *My Little Chickadee* and *Never Give a Sucker an Even Break*.

W. C. Fields

Benjamin Franklin (1706–1790), one of the most esteemed of all Americans, helped edit the Declaration of Independence and draft the U.S. Constitution. Franklin was born in Boston, Massachusetts. By age 15, he was writing articles for his brother's newspaper. In 1723, he moved to Philadelphia, where he founded the nation's first public library. He also bought the *Pennsylvania Gazette* and turned it into a witty and informative newspaper. Franklin later began publishing *Poor Richard's Almanack*, a wildly popular book that was full of advice. Franklin was also a scientist, famous for his electricity experiments and for inventing the Franklin stove. During and after the Revolutionary War, Franklin served as a diplomat in England and France, where his wit, intelligence, and integrity made him very popular.

Robert Fulton (1765–1815) of Lancaster County built the first efficient steamboat. One of Fulton's early designs was for a submarine, which he tried to sell to France. In 1807, his steamboat *Clermont* made a historic run from New York City to Albany, New York. This proved that steamships were trustworthy, and he received a patent for the invention. Fulton also designed the first steam-powered warship for the U.S. government.

Martha Graham (1894–1991) was the most influential figure in modern dance. As a dancer and choreographer, she favored stark staging and an expressive, dramatic style. Graham believed dance should use the body to convey true inner feelings. If the emotion being expressed was anger, jealousy, or fear, the movements might not be pretty. Graham's dances include *Appalachian Spring* and *Acrobats of God*. She was born in Allegheny.

Martha Graham

Milton Hershey (1857–1945) founded the company that became famous for Hershey's chocolate bars and Hershey's Kisses. He started his career as an apprentice candy maker in Lancaster. He eventually began making his own caramels and then chocolate. Today, the company he founded remains one of the world's leading candy makers. Hershey was born in Derry Church, which was renamed Hershey after he established his business there.

Reggie Jackson (1946–   ) is baseball's sixth-leading home run hitter of all time. Jackson spent most of his career with the Oakland A's and the New York Yankees. He led the Yankees to two World Series championships.

Jackson's clutch play at the end of the season, particularly hitting four consecutive home runs in the 1977 World Series, earned him the nickname Mr. October. Jackson, who was elected to the National Baseball Hall of Fame in 1993, was born in Wyncote.

Reggie Jackson

Gene Kelly (1912–1996) was an actor, dancer, and choreographer famous for his exuberant, athletic dancing in such films as *Singin' in the Rain* and *An American in Paris*. Kelly began dancing as a child, studying at his mother's dance school. He had already earned acclaim for his performance in *Pal Joey* on Broadway when he made his film debut in 1942 in *For Me and My Gal*. Kelly was born in Pittsburgh.

Grace Kelly (1929–1982), a Philadelphia native, was a well-known actress who became Princess Grace of Monaco. The elegant and sophisticated actress began her career on Broadway but soon began making films. She appeared in such classics as *High Noon*, *Rear Window*, and *Dial M for Murder* and earned an Academy Award for her role in *The Country Girl*. In 1956, Grace Kelly married Prince Rainier of Monaco. Although her career was soaring, she retired from acting.

George C. Marshall (1880–1959) was a soldier and diplomat born in Uniontown. Marshall was educated at the Virginia Military Institute. By

George C. Marshall

1939, he had risen to the rank of general and been appointed the U.S. Army chief of staff. In 1947, Marshall became the U.S. secretary of state. Perhaps his most lasting legacy was the Marshall Plan, a program of economic assistance to help rebuild war-torn western Europe. Marshall's efforts in helping Europe recover from World War II earned him the 1953 Nobel Prize for peace.

Margaret Mead (1901–1978), a pioneering anthropologist best known for her studies of South Pacific cultures, was born in Philadelphia. In such books as *Coming of Age in Samoa*, Mead studied how children become part of their culture and how culture affects personality. For more than 40 years, she was a curator at the American Museum of Natural History in New York.

Stan Musial (1920–   ) of Donora was one of the greatest baseball players in history. Musial played for the St. Louis Cardinals from 1941 to 1963 and later became the Cardinals' manager. An exceptionally smart and consistent hitter, he won the National League batting championship seven times and the Most Valuable Player Award three times. He also played in an amazing 24 all-star games. Musial was inducted into the National Baseball Hall of Fame in 1969.

Arnold Palmer (1929–   ), a Latrobe native, is a legend of golf. Palmer was the first golfer to win the Masters championship four times and the first to win $1 million in prize money. His winning ways and charismatic, go-for-broke personality attracted legions of fans, who became known as Arnie's Army.

Robert E. Peary (1856–1920) is generally credited with being the first explorer to reach the North Pole. Peary began his career in the navy, participating in surveys in Central America. His attention eventually turned northward, and he explored much of Greenland. Peary made several unsuccessful attempts to reach the North Pole before finally achieving his goal in 1909. Peary was born in Cresson.

Will Smith (1968–   ), a Philadelphia native, is a popular actor and rap singer. Smith began performing as a rap singer at age 12. He soon began calling himself Fresh Prince, and he and his partner, DJ Jazzy Jeff, made several hit records while still in high school. With his amiable, engaging personality, Smith was soon starring in a television show called *The Fresh Prince of Bel Air*. Today, he is a leading film actor, having starred in such blockbusters as *Men in Black* and *Independence Day*.

Gertrude Stein (1874–1946) was a writer famous for her experimental style, which used simple language and very little punctuation. Her works include *Three Lives* and *The Autobiography of Alice B. Toklas*. Stein moved to Paris, France, in 1903 and lived there the rest of her life. In Paris, she was at the center of an intellectual circle that included novelist Ernest Hemingway and painters Pablo Picasso and Henri Matisse. Stein was an important early promoter of these and other modern artists and amassed an impressive collection of their work. She was born in Allegheny.

Gertrude Stein

James Stewart (1908–1997), an actor from Indiana, Pennsylvania, was known for his honest characters and hesitant drawl. His many movies include *It's a Wonderful Life*, *Mr. Smith Goes to Washington*, and *Vertigo*. He earned an Academy Award in 1941 for his performance in *The Philadelphia Story*. In 1985, Stewart was awarded the Presidential Medal of Freedom, the U.S. government's highest civilian honor.

Ida M. Tarbell (1857–1944) was a journalist and a leading figure in the muckraking movement, which tried to expose corruption and abuse in business and politics. She is most famous for writing a book carefully documenting the business practices of the Standard Oil Company, which led to a government suit against the giant company. Tarbell also wrote a highly regarded biography of President Abraham Lincoln. She was born in Erie County.

John Updike (1932–   ) is a prominent novelist who writes about the dark side of suburban life. Among his many carefully crafted novels are *The Centaur*, which won the 1963 National Book Award, and *The Witches of Eastwick*. He is perhaps best known for a series of novels that follow a disillusioned man named Harry "Rabbit" Angstrom through the decades, including *Rabbit Is Rich* and *Rabbit at Rest*, both of which won Pulitzer Prizes. Updike was born in Reading.

Honus Wagner (1874–1955), who spent most of his career with the Pittsburgh Pirates, is considered the greatest shortstop in baseball history, both an excellent hitter and an amazing fielder. Swift and powerful, he was the National League batting champion eight times and the stolen base champion five times. He hit over .300 17 years in a row, a National League record. In 1936, he became one of the first five players elected to the Baseball Hall of Fame. Wagner, nicknamed the Flying

Dutchman because of his speed and Pennsylvania Dutch background, was born in Mansfield.

Andy Warhol (1928-1987), one of the most talked-about American artists of the 20th century, was a leader in the pop art movement, which took its subjects from popular culture. He is best remembered for painting subjects such as Campbell's soup cans and the actress Marilyn Monroe. Warhol also made experimental motion pictures, including *Empire*, an eight-hour film of the Empire State Building in which nothing changes but the light. The Andy Warhol Museum, the largest museum in the United States devoted to a single artist, is in his hometown of Pittsburgh.

Daniel Hale Williams (1858–1931), an African-American physician from Hollidaysburg, performed the world's first successful open-heart surgery. Williams received his medical degree from Chicago Medical College, which is now part of Northwestern University. He later helped found Provident Hospital, the first hospital in Chicago to accept patients regardless of race and to have blacks on staff. At Provident in 1893, Williams made medical history by repairing a heart with a knife wound. Williams performed surgery at hospitals throughout Chicago and taught anatomy at Northwestern.

Daniel Hale Williams

August Wilson (1945–   ) is a leading playwright whose work has chronicled African-American life in the 20th century. His plays, such as *Fences* and *The Piano Lesson*, both Pulitzer Prize winners, are noted for their humor, lively dialogue, and mixture of realism and fantasy. Wilson was born in Pittsburgh.

Gettysburg National Military Park

TOUR THE STATE

Gettysburg National Military Park (Gettysburg) Few people leave unmoved by a tour of the battlefield where more than 50,000 soldiers died. You can also visit the cemetery where President Abraham Lincoln made his famous address.

Hawk Mountain Sanctuary (Kempton) Although most people visit the sanctuary to see some of the thousands of birds of prey that pass through the region each autumn, it is also worth a stop for its wildflowers and hiking trails.

State Museum of Pennsylvania (Harrisburg) Ancient forests, ancient rocks, ancient peoples—you'll learn all about Pennsylvania's past at this fine museum.

Rockville Bridge (Harrisburg) At 3,820 feet long, this span over the Susquehanna River is one of the world's largest stone arch bridges.

Hershey's Chocolate World (Hershey) There's no escaping chocolate in the town of Hershey—even the streetlights are shaped like Hershey's Kisses. A ride through Chocolate World will explain how the nation's favorite candy is made. At the end you get a free sample.

The People's Place (Intercourse) At this center dedicated to the Pennsylvania Dutch, you can sit down to school lessons given to Amish children, try your hand at the turn signals in an Amish carriage, and admire an extraordinary collection of quilts.

Valley Forge National Historical Park (King of Prussia) At this park you can imagine what it was like to have lived through a frigid winter during the Revolutionary War while also enjoying one of the most scenic parts of Pennsylvania.

Grand Carousel (Lahaska) You may want to hop on a carved tiger when you ride this beautiful 1922 carousel.

Independence National Historical Park (Philadelphia) Within just a few square blocks, you can see Independence Hall, where the Declaration of Independence was adopted; Carpenters' Hall, where the First Continental Congress met; the Liberty Bell; and Christ Church, which was attended by George Washington and other Founding Fathers.

Philadelphia Zoo (Philadelphia) Look a lemur in the eye, roar with tigers, and pet a cuddly lamb at the oldest zoo in the United States.

Johnstown Flood Museum (Johnstown) This fascinating museum chronicles the disastrous flood of 1889 that destroyed the bustling city of Johnstown and killed more than two thousand people.

Fallingwater (Mill Run) One of the most famous buildings in the country, this house built over a waterfall is one of architect Frank Lloyd Wright's masterpieces.

Monongahela Incline (Pittsburgh) A trip on this trolley that climbs the side of a hill provides a spectacular view of Pittsburgh.

Little League Baseball Museum (Williamsport) At this museum, you can take a swing in the batting cage and then watch your style on video. You can also watch highlights of past Little League World Series and learn about former Little Leaguers who made it big.

Pine Creek Gorge (Wellsboro) Known as the Grand Canyon of Pennsylvania, this majestic 1,100-foot-deep canyon is an ideal spot for boating, hiking, horseback riding, and skiing.

Niagara (Erie) This beautiful replica of the *Niagara*, Commodore Oliver Hazard Perry's flagship when he achieved his famous victory over the British during the War of 1812, was built in the 1980s.

Presque Isle State Park (Erie) A visit to Presque Isle might include relaxing on sandy beaches, spying migrating birds, or bicycling through lush forests. But no matter what you do, end your day watching the skies, for Presque Isle is the best place to watch sunsets over Lake Erie.

FUN FACTS

The Hershey plant in Hershey, Pennsylvania, is the world's largest chocolate factory.

Edwin Drake drilled the first successful oil well in the nation in 1859, near Titusville.

Philadelphia has been the site of many firsts. The colonies' first botanic garden was founded in Philadelphia by John Bartram in 1728. It is still in existence. The first circulating library in the colonies was established in Philadelphia in 1731. The first bank in the present-day United States was the Bank of North America, which began operating in Philadelphia in 1781. And in 1784 Philadelphia's *Pennsylvania Packet and General Advertiser*, became America's first daily newspaper.

FIND OUT MORE

To find out more about Pennsylvania, look for the following titles in your school or public library:

GENERAL STATE BOOKS

Swain, Gwenyth. *Pennsylvania.* Minneapolis: Lerner Publications, 1994.

Thompson, Kathleen. *Pennsylvania.* Austin, TX: Raintree/Steck-Vaughan, 1996.

BOOKS ABOUT PEOPLE OR HISTORY

Ammon, Richard, *Growing Up Amish.* New York: Atheneum, 1989.

Anderson, Peter. *Gifford Pinchot: America's Forester.* New York: Franklin Watts, 1995.

Bial, Raymond. *Amish House.* Boston: Houghton Mifflin, 1993.

Burby, Liza N. *Rachel Carson: Writer and Environmentalist.* New York: Powerkids Press, 1997.

Haskins, James. *Bayard Rustin: Behind the Scenes of the Civil Rights Movement.* New York: Hyperion Books for Children, 1997.

Kaye, Judith. *The Life of Daniel Hale Williams* New York: Twenty-First Century Books, 1993.

Meyer, Susan E. *First Impressions: Mary Cassatt.* New York: Harry N. Abrams, 1990.

Quakenbush, Robert. *Stop the Presses, Nellie's Got a Scoop!* New York: Simon and Schuster Books for Young Readers, 1992.

Stefoff, Rebecca. *William Penn.* Philadelphia: Chelsea House Publications, 1998.

Stein, R. Conrad. *The Story of Valley Forge.* Chicago: Children's Press, 1985.

Venezia, Mike. *Andy Warhol.* Chicago: Children's Press, 1996.

INTERNET SITES

To find out more about what is going on in Pennsylvania today, check out the following Internet sites:

The State Home Page: http://www.state.pa.us/
    This site will give you loads of information on Pennsylvania and will connect you to links that explore special interests.

The Pennsylvania Ski Guide: http://home.earthlink.net/~eschr/skiguide.html
    This website gives a display of all the state's major ski areas. You can get directions to each ski area, find out what you can do there besides ski, and learn the current weather and snow conditions.

INDEX

Page numbers for charts, graphs, and illustrations are in boldface.